Direct Response Fund Raising

The NSFRE/Wiley Fund Development Series

Beyond Fund Raising: New Strategies for Nonprofit Innovation and Investment by Kay Sprinkel Grace

The Complete Guide to Fund-Raising Management by Stanley Weinstein

Critical Issues in Fund Raising edited by Dwight F. Burlingame

The Fund Raiser's Guide to the Internet by Michael Johnston

Ethical Decision Making in Fund Raising by Marilyn Fischer

Fund Raising: Evaluating and Managing the Fund Development Process, Second Edition by James M. Greenfield

Fund-Raising Cost Effectiveness: A Self-Assessment Workbook by James M. Greenfield

International Fund Raising for Not-for-Profits: A Country by Country Profile by Thomas Harris

The Nonprofit Handbook: Fund Raising, Second Edition edited by James M. Greenfield

Nonprofit Investment Policies: A Practical Guide to Creation and Implementation by Robert P. Fry, Jr.

The NSFRE Fundraising Dictionary by National Society of Fund Raising Executives

Planned Giving Simplified: The Gift, the Giver, and the Gift Planner by Robert F. Sharpe, Sr.

The Universal Benefits of Volunteering: A Practical Workbook for Nonprofit Organizations, Volunteers, and Corporations by Walter Pidgeon

Direct Response Fund Raising

Mastering New Trends for Results

Michael Johnston

JOHN WILEY & SONS, INC.
NEW YORK / CHICHESTER / WEINHEIM / BRISBANE / SINGAPORE / TORONTO

This publication is designed to provide accurate and authoritative information in regard to the subject matter covered. It is sold with the understanding that the publisher is not engaged in rendering legal, accounting, or other professional services. If legal advice or other expert assistance is required, the services of a competent professional person should be sought.

Library of Congress Cataloging-in-Publication Data

Johnston, Michael W., 1963-
   Direct response fund raising: mastering new trends for results / by Michael Johnston.
      p. cm.— (Wiley nonprofit law, finance, and management series)
   ISBN 0-471-38024-5 (cloth/CD-ROM: alk. paper)
   1. Fund raising. 2. Direct-mail fund raising. I. Title. II. Series.
HV41.2 .J63 2000
658.15'224—dc21

00-025340

Printed in the United States of America.

10 9 8 7 6 5 4 3 2 1

▼ About the Editor

Michael Johnston, President of Hewitt and Johnston Consultants, a full-service fund-raising consulting firm based in Toronto, Canada, was a senior consultant from 1988 to 1991 with Stephen Thomas Associates, the first fund-raising firm in Canada to work exclusively with nonprofit organizations. In 1991 he was a fund-raising consultant for the Australian Labor Party in Canberra and Melbourne.

Michael has worked with hundreds of nonprofit organizations—ranging from third world development organizations, to hospitals, community centers, and peace and disarmament groups—in Canada, the United States, and the United Kingdom.

Michael is a past board member, and current member, of the National Society of Fund-Raising Executives (NSFRE) and sits on the NSFRE's Volunteer Online Council in Alexandria, Virginia. He has been a past member of the Ethics Committee of the Canadian Society of Fund-Raising Executives and was a volunteer fund-raising leader with the United Way in its Management Assistance Program, where he assisted agencies in developing strategic fund-raising solutions. Michael is the author of two books: *The Fund Raiser's Guide to the Internet* and *The Nonprofit Guide to the Internet,* both published by John Wiley & Sons.

▼ About the Contributors

Jeff Gignac, as President and Founder of JMG Solutions, has been working with a variety of charities since 1992. An expert in assisting with the technical challenges involved in fund-raising, he is unequaled in Canada with over 400 database implementations behind him. Not only is the breadth of his experience unique, he is more than a "techie"—by looking at everyone's "big picture," he has taken time to listen and learn. Jeff understands fund-raising and prospect research as well as the many challenges faced by charities today. In addition to training, Jeff has performed data conversions, database clean-ups, procedure documentation, and donation process improvement. Together with his new wife, Pamela, projects have included the British Red Cross, the Prince's Youth Business Trust, the Canadian Red Cross, the Baycrest Centre Foundation, the Children's Hospital of Eastern Ontario, the Calgary Zoo, the Ontario March of Dimes, Centennial College, and the Canadian Breast Cancer Foundation. For further information visit www.jmgsolutions.com.

Fran Jacobowitz, CFRE, Executive Vice President of Lautman & Company, has consulted for clients such as the United States Holocaust Memorial Museum, the Smithsonian's National Museum of the American Indian, the Japanese American National Museum, Defenders of Wildlife, AARP Andrus Foundation, the National Foundation for Cancer Research and Meharry Medical College.

She is a Certified Fund Raising Executive (CFRE), a member of the Board of Directors of the Washington, DC, chapter of NSFRE, and the chapter's Vice President for Membership.

Prior to serving as Vice President of Lautman & Company (formerly Oram Group Marketing), she worked at the Smithsonian Institution's Resident Associate Program, where she was responsible for membership development and marketing.

Trained in direct-mail and marketing techniques at Wunderman, Ricotta & Kline, the direct marketing division of Young and Rubicam, Ms. Jacobowitz has more than 20 years of experience in direct marketing and strategic planning for consumer, business-to-business, governmental, nonprofit, and fund-raising clients.

Kay Partney Lautman, CFRE, is President of Lautman & Company, a fund-raising firm in Washington, DC, specializing in membership and donor development.

She has developed successful direct-mail campaigns for organizations including the Vietnam Veterans Memorial, the United States Holocaust Memorial Museum, and the American Society for the Prevention of Cruelty to Animals.

For 18 years she was President of Oram Group Marketing, and prior to that she was Associate Director of the World Wildlife Fund. In 1985 the Washington DC Chapter of NSFRE named Ms. Lautman Outstanding Fund Raising Executive. In 1994 the Women's Direct Response Group named her Woman of the Year, and in 1996 she was given a Lifetime Achievement Award by the Nonprofit Council of the Direct Marketing Association (DMA).

Ms. Lautman is coauthor, with Hank Goldstein, of the best-seller *Dear Friend: Mastering the Art of Direct Mail Fund Raising,* published by The Taft Group, and is a frequent speaker at fund-raising seminars and conferences.

David Love is Principal Consultant for Stephen Thomas Consulting (STC). STC is a new division of Stephen Thomas (ST), Canada's leading direct marketing firm specializing in charitable organizations.

For 20 years previously, David was Vice President of World Wildlife Fund Canada, responsible for coordinating all fund-raising and communications for WWF.

In his early days as a consultant, David has advised clients on planned giving, major donor campaigns, major donor clubs, direct-response television, monthly giving programs, and direct dialogue, among other things. He revels in his new job bringing skills and ideas developed in over 30 years of raising money to some of Canada's most worthy organizations.

Along the way, David is meeting a host of exceptionally talented people working hard to make the world a better place. From these people, he learns new things almost every day that he can pass on to his clients.

Judith Nichols is an Oregon-based development consultant with a variety of not-for-profit clients across the United States and in Australia, South America, Canada, the United Kingdom, and Europe. She specializes in helping charities to understand and fund-raise effectively from today's diversified audiences.

Dr. Nichols has been a featured speaker and trainer at numerous conferences, workshops, and symposia in the United States, Europe, and Canada. Her books include: *Transforming Fund Raising; Lessons from Abroad:*

Fresh Ideas from Fund-Raising Experts in the United Kingdom; Global Demographics: Fund Raising for a New World; and *Growing from Good to Great: Positioning Your Fund Raising Efforts for BIG Gains.* She is also the author of *Pinpointing Affluence: Increasing Your Share of Major Donor Dollars; Targeted Fund Raising: Defining and Refining Your Development Strategy; Changing Demographics: Fund Raising in the 1990s;* and *By the Numbers: Using Demographics and Psychographics for Business Growth in the 1990s.*

Jason Potts, Head of New Media, Burnett Associates, London, England, has worked in direct marketing for eight years. In his four and a half years at Burnett Associates, he has worked as a creative on interactive and response-driven campaigns for dozens of leading not-for-profit organizations.

He is a regular speaker on the future of new media and convergence in the social marketing sector on platforms in Europe and all over the world. Recognized as a practitioner at the leading edge of his profession with numerous published papers, he is currently contributing new media chapters to several forthcoming direct-response books.

As Head of New Media at Burnett Associates, he has put together online strategies and implementation for many high-profile clients, including the multi–award-winning fund-raising site for Amnesty International UK.

Mal Warwick, a consultant, author, and public speaker, has been involved in the not-for-profit sector for more than 35 years. He is the Founder and Chairman of a full-service direct-mail fund-raising firm, Mal Warwick & Associates (Berkeley, Calif.), and Cofounder of Share Group, Inc. (Somerville, Mass.), a telephone fund-raising agency. Mal has written or edited 10 books of interest to fund-raisers, including *The Five Strategies for Fundraising Success* (Jossey-Bass, 1999) and the classics, *Revolution in the Mailbox* and *How to Write Successful Fundraising Letters.* He also edits a newsletter, *Successful Direct Mail & Telephone Fundraising.* His clients have included many of the nation's largest and most distinguished nonprofit organizations as well as six Democratic presidential candidates. Together with his colleagues, he has raised more than $500 million during 20 years as a fund-raiser.

▼ Acknowledgments

With an edited anthology, the editor is at the mercy of so many other people: the contributors, the publisher, the support staff, and those dreaded production windows.

Luckily for me, the people who made this book come about were committed and wonderful individuals. I was warned that editing an anthology would be like being a lion tamer armed with only a whip and chair.

I'm happy to say I never really had to use the whip or the chair (perhaps only on myself) to make deadlines and get the material poured into this book.

I have to start off with a special thank you to Martha Cooley. She's supported me through the writing of two books other than this one in the last two years, and I can honestly tell you that this product wouldn't have happened without her. She kept me to deadlines with supportive words and useful insights on the shape of the material. She rarely used deadline threats.

What was most amazing wasn't her attention to detail but the fact she had many other books to shepherd to their finished form, yet I always felt like mine was the only book she was working on. Thanks so much, Martha.

The contributors are the soul of this book. Their perspectives, ideas, and sharing make this anthology a useful resource for fund-raisers anywhere in the world. I asked each of them to write on a particular topic, and they all picked up the challenge. I especially want to thank Jeff Gignac, who put the finishing touches on his chapter while he was running a temperature of 102 and could barely speak.

There were so many nonprofit organizations that made the generous contribution of agreeing to put their fund-raising examples in this book. I can't name them all here but you'll see their material in the book and I thank them all. This sector thrives when we share and learn from one another.

We can't afford to have market research and testing conducted by individual nonprofit organizations because our budgets are limited. This isn't the commercial sector. That's why a shared resource like this one is so important to our work as fund-raisers.

A number of expert fund-raisers—Graham Knope, for example—gave their time and expertise for in-depth interviews. Thanks to everyone, and I want you to know that I owe you a drink when I visit your home city or town.

In my two other books two dear people were integral to my work—my good friend George Irish and my twin brother, Mark Johnston. Once again George helped immensely, and the graphics you see in this book are his doing. Mark continued to be the grit in the oyster—asking why I wasn't working on the book on a beautiful Saturday. Though his persistence could be irritating, I think he pushed me to work that extra amount here and there to finish the book in the form I wanted.

There's one special person who really organized this book and ensured that we gathered all the permissions, soothed ruffled feathers, and kept the book organized from my end. Without Gordon Baker's help, my publisher would have received a poorly organized manuscript. Gordon made order out of chaos and subsequently made this book better for you, the reader.

Finally, I want to thank my good friend Karen for keeping me inspired by life, thankful for good health, and reminding me that a smile is sometimes better than anything else.

Contents

CONTENTS

▼ Preface

I can't think of how many times I've been sitting in my rather uncomfortable chair in my second floor office—stumped by some direct response fund-raising problem. Sometimes I've been unable to come up with a good lead to a letter, stymied for good package idea, or in need of help on direct response donor demographics.

Frustrated, I'll throw a lazy glance out the window and focus on the green vines surrounding my window or maybe absently watch the neighbor's ginger cat balance on the unsteady trellis in the back yard—anything to avoid finding a solution to a particular direct response fund-raising problem.

I'll continue to look out the window, and around the office, until my eyes come across a row of direct response (or related) fund-raising books. I'll look at the titles and then look at the names of the authors . . . Mal Warwick, Kay Lautman, Judith Nichols, Con Squires, Jerry Huntsinger, and a number of others.

Invariably, I'll get up from my chair (not a hard thing to do with an uncomfortable seat) and grab one or two of the books and start flipping.

'Ah hah!'

'Ooh, look at that!'

'I would have never though of that.'

'That's exactly what I need.'

The best books in the field always show me what's working (and what's not) and give me ample ideas, guidance and advice to make my clients more money. I can't think of how many fund-raising problems were solved by a read through an excellent direct response fund-raising book.

That's what I set out to do with this book—give the reader a book that they can grab off their shelves and find inspiration and guidance to do more effective direct response fund-raising.

I can tell you it wasn't easy. I wanted to get some of the best practioners in the field and ask if they'd contribute to this book. I'm so glad so many of them said yes and then got down to work. I can't say enough about well-known practioners and seasoned authors like Mal Warwick, Kay Lautman, and Judith Nichols, who all made generous contributions to this book. But any anthology needs a wide range of contributors and that's why I've added longtime, well-respected practioners like David Love and

Fran Jackobiwitz to the mix. Finally, what would any anthology be without the young bucks. Jason Potts and Jeff Gignac provide insight and energetic contributions to this book as well.

Together, these contributors provide insight, examples and expertise on a wide range of direct response fund-raising issues.

But this isn't a simple exposition on current practices—with samples and results—because I believe there are big changes afoot in the direct response industry.

The Internet, CD-ROMs, computer databases, and a number of other technological factors are changing the way that direct response fund-raising is being conducted now and in the future. Please read Jason's chapter especially to see how New Media is being put into the direct response mix.

However, it's too facile to say that new technologies will radically change the way we conduct direct response fund-raising. Mal Warwick's introduction provides a powerful argument that many of the principles we've always used in direct response fund-raising will still remain constant in the near and distant future. The techniques and some of the delivery mediums will change, but the power of a good story will always be important!

Kay Lautman and Fran Jackobowitz's chapter provides a precise look at direct mail testing and makes the case that the more things change the more they stay the same—with an especially valuable reminder that every nonprofit organization must continue to test direct response findings and results—no matter the medium.

I believe that as you flip through this book you'll notice that the contributors don't forget the past while they analyze the present and make some brave, calculated guesses about the future.

Nonprofit organizations cannot make the best decisions on their direct response fund-raising without being informed. Every nonprofit organization has limited financial and human resource capital to spend on direct response fund-raising. Every decision needs to be the right one (well, not every decision, we can all learn from our mistakes), but almost every one!

At the same time that nonprofit direct response fund-raising is becoming increasingly powerful, effective and precise because of improvements in database technology and a number of other technological breakthroughs, it is also becoming more expensive. That's why every nonprofit needs to make the best decisions (tactical or strategic) when it comes to direct response fund-raising.

The next time you're stuck on exactly how you can improve your direct response fund-raising program—and you're staring out your window, I hope your eye might land on this book and you'll pick it up and flip through it.

You won't be able to accurately predict the future because as I like to remember the wise words of an 800-year-old Jedi Master—Yoda—who once said, "Difficult to see. Always in motion is the future."

But maybe, just maybe, you'll find the solution you need to add something new to your direct response fund-raising mix that you've never used before (e.g., an Internet campaign or e-mail solicitation campaign) or you'll see an example from the old media mix (e.g., direct mail or the telephone) that reinvigorates what you're already doing.

I sincerely hope this book catches your eye the next time your gaze wanders out the window . . .

Mike Johnston

Direct Response Fund Raising

Introduction
Heads Up! Eyes on the Future!

Mal Warwick

When I launched my career in direct mail fund-raising in the late 1970s, I marveled at the advanced technology at my disposal: a sleek IBM Selectric II typewriter on which I drafted copy for my clients' appeals. Of course, I had to retype each appeal again and again until I got it right.

Now, as we open our eyes on the 21st century, I shuttle draft copy across the continent via e-mail, giving colleagues and clients alike the opportunity to edit the appeals themselves—and return them to me instantaneously.

The last two decades have seen tremendous changes in communications technology as it relates to fund-raising writing.

So, how could I know what the copy development process will look like 20 or 30 years from now? Will I still "type" on a keyboard? Will sounds and visual images loom larger in conveying an appeal?

Two decades ago my clients and I relied exclusively on conventional printing processes to reproduce our appeals—fast-moving web presses for large-volume jobs; smaller, sheet-fed presses for specialty items. Nowadays, I have a great many options, including a variety of laser-printed and ink-jetted formats, some of which I can manage in my own office.

In just the last 20 years, we've gone from producing high-quality direct response packages on the plant floor to the home office.

Considering this transformation of location and capital investment, how will we deliver our messages two decades from now? Will printing take place exclusively on the "back end," in the recipient's home or office, if at all? Will paper still be commonly used? Will every appeal be so custom-tailored to each individual addressee that it will be truly unique?

On my maiden voyages into the sea of direct response, I had exactly two ways to "involve" donors and prospects through my mailings: (1) through the reply device, sometimes elaborated with a questionnaire, a petition, or postcard; and (2) a front-end premium. Today, by contrast, just 20 years later, I can encourage responses on a Web site, by e-mail, or via a toll-free telephone number as well as by "snail" mail. I can invite major donors to join me in a nationwide conference call. I can stage a live on-line chat led by the executive director. I can phone donors and offer them the opportunity to be "patched through" to their congress member's office—or to trigger the delivery of a personalized fax or e-mail protest. I can offer custom-tailored messages on a toll-free inbound hot line using interactive voice response (without a human operator).

Technological changes have given the direct-response fund-raiser more than just paper options to get donors involved.

I've moved from paper to the Internet in just 20 years, so what will be my options for donor involvement 20 years from now?

Okay, let's get something straight right off the bat: The answer to all these questions is: Nobody knows.

A Cloudy Crystal Ball

I begin with the premise that it is impossible to predict the future. Yes, you read that right: *impossible,* not merely challenging or laborious. For example, consider what we know about the prospects for change in just three of the innumerable variables that may govern the course of human life on this planet in the 21st century.

1.   Chances are, leaders have never heard of it. It's now the subject of increasing attention in scientific and engineering laboratories around the world. "It" is known by the tongue-twisting label "molecular nanotechnology." It's science's new way to manipulate matter at the atomic level—to realize the alchemists' dream, creating useful things from such stuff as water, sand, and stone. Molecular nanotechnology is believed to have the potential to spawn self-replicating "machines" so tiny that they can navigate the human bloodstream to combat disease at the molecular level—or repair a broken body. The field also has the potential to eliminate the need for conventional manufacturing—or, critics say, to unleash uncontrollable forces that will consume all life on Earth. Critics point out that humans are having difficulty controlling the mutation of natural viruses, let alone artificial, self-replicating machines of the same size and spawning potential of viruses. How will we combat nantechnology gone astray?

2.   There is a scientific consensus that our world is warming and the sea level rising as a result of the cumulative impact of human activity on Earth. Already, the polar ice caps are melting, the seasons are changing,

and wildlife habitats are shifting in response. The very survival of small island nations is threatened. Who today can predict how soon or how successfully our government and corporate leaders will push for the lifestyle changes necessary to slow the advent of global climate change? Are the world's major cities doomed? After all, 80 percent of them are near a coastline and vulnerable to rising seas. On the other hand, 10 years ago the ozone layer was found to be thinning dangerously over the polar ice caps, but now they are healing themselves. It appears that Mother Nature may be beyond our ability to understand and control.

   3.   Some observers of the computer industry are beginning to speak about the prospects for what author Ray Kurzweil called "spiritual machines"—self-aware computers with intellectual capacity far surpassing that of the brightest human being . . . and eventually exceeding the collective intelligence of all humans on the planet. Kurzweil asserts that the equivalent of a desktop machine available today for $1,000 will put human intellectual ability to shame by the year 2030. What might this portend for our schools, our professional lives, our clumsy attempts to govern ourselves?

   Who among us would be so brave as to say that the prospects for the nonprofit sector, for philanthropy, and for fund-raising will not be radically affected if manufacturing is no longer necessary . . . if we're forced to abandon our cities . . . or if computers surpass human intelligence?

   Yet those are just three areas of uncertainty the human species faces as we peer off into the mists of the future—and we habitually view these variables in isolation from one another. But developments in any of these areas will surely influence what happens in any other field. And one doesn't have to stretch one's mind very far to come up with a host of other imponderable factors—from overpopulation, to biotechnology, to the emergence of terrifying new diseases, to the growing scarcity of fresh water, to the search for extraterrestrial intelligence. In any one of these spheres of human endeavor, an unpredictable turn of events might at any time have a profound and irreversible effect on our lives.

   So anyone who pretends to know what the future holds in store is a little bit nuts.

Predicting Future Changes

Now, I've been called much worse than "nuts," so I'm going to take a stab at predicting the future of direct-response fund-raising, anyway. After all, you paid good money for this book, so you want to get something useful from it—or at least entertaining, no?

In any case, I'd prefer not to think all life on Earth is doomed, or that computers are destined to outsmart us, or that New York and L.A. will slip under the ocean's waves. And I suspect that private voluntary organizations will have a large role to play throughout the 21st century, regardless of how the future unfolds.

So here are the six essentially new characteristics I believe direct-response fund-raising systems may share approximately 20 years from now. The systems will be:

1. *Individualized.* Our appeals will not just be "personalized" but "individualized." By and large, we won't be dealing with donor file "segments" any more but with individuals—responding to their unique, personal interests and capabilities. We've always asked donors for personalized information, but because of the labor needed to utilize survey data, we've never truly individualized our appeals. (How many boxes full of donor surveys went unopened in the past?) However, with new technologies we'll know a lot more about our donors and be able to use the information immediately—facts and figures gathered through more frequent surveys and questionnaires. And these future information management systems will be capable of storing, organizing, and analyzing much more data than most charities now find it practical to retain.

2. *Multisensory.* Our appeals will use forms of what today are called "multimedia" technologies. We won't be limited to paper, or to voice communications, or to prerecorded sounds or video images. A single fund-raising appeal might consist of sights, sounds, and data, and be delivered—separately or simultaneously—through several communications channels: a wall screen, perhaps, with full-motion sound and video; or a pocket communicator bearing a simplified, two-dimensional version; or a hardcopy printout resembling what today we call a fax. Donors will choose which method they prefer, and open the appeal up when and where they wish, suiting the mood or constraints of the moment or merely following long-established preferences for one format or another.

3. *Information rich.* On-line databases and super–high-speed data transmission will permit us to make veritable mountains of information available to every prospect or donor—and the demands of competition will force us to do so. Meanwhile, flexible database management software will permit all prospects and all donors to select precisely those bits of information they want—and not one word or one image more. Just as I

program my communications system to preselect news stories I'm likely to find interesting, my clients' donors will teach their own software "agents" to sift through mountains of information—including newsletters, bulletins, annual reports, and special appeals from nonprofits—to select those things that match their own interests or circumstances.

4. *Real time.* Within two decades, real-time transactions will be common in direct response fund-raising. "Real-time" is computer jargon for "right now." For example, by authorizing a gift in the course of an on-line videoconference with her favorite charity, a donor may instantaneously transmit funds from her bank account to the charity—even before the conference is over. The response curves we measure today in weeks and months may be viewed in terms of hours or even minutes 20 years from now. Already nonprofit organizations are working with financial institutions to offer automatic bank account deductions on-line, and they are running on-line fund-raising campaigns that last only one or two weeks.

5. *Interactive.* Donors will actively participate, not just in selecting the amount and the format of the information they receive, but the role they'll play in the life and work of the charities they support. Today's dedicated donor hot lines will become multimedia gateways that offer donors a multitude of new options: to participate in the latter-day equivalent of focus group research, for example; to share their specialized expertise with program staff; or to integrate what they're learning from us into ongoing educational programs. Both two-way and small-group communications will be an integral part of the process—freeing fund-raisers from the constraints of time and geography and permitting the development of rich and rewarding relationships with donors they may never meet face-to-face.

6. *Communal.* The nonprofits that flourish in the fast-moving environment of the 21st century will be those that provide their supporters with the experience of community. Today's rapidly multiplying computer networks, e-mail systems, chat rooms, local-access cable TV, video teleconferencing, and e-mail facilities foreshadow the integrated technologies of the 21st century. Within 20 years, charities will be able to engage thousands of their donors in a profoundly personal and meaningful way—simultaneously, and over great physical distances. Meanwhile, as individuals, many donors will find that the nearly instantaneous, broadband communications of the new era permit them to turn a shared commitment to a charity's work into personal relationships with many of their fellow donors. Just as users of today's converging technologies are forming "virtual communities," often spanning continents and oceans, donors by the thousands eventually may be able to join with a charity's other constituents—staff, board, clients, alumni—in shared access to the daily experience of the charity's work. How? Through a latter-day equivalent of "personal" ads in the newsletters or public forums on the communications network of the future. That experience and the personal relationships that result may enrich daily life in the 21st century for tens of millions of people.

What the Future Will Not Change

Of all the forms and modes of fund-raising, direct response is without doubt the most responsive to changing technologies. Some of these changes—or other, comparable developments—seem inevitable to me, given the velocity of new-product development in today's communications industries. But there's much more to direct response than just the techniques and formats we use to deliver our messages. There are fundamental factors, rooted in knowledge of human behavior and the accumulated wisdom of the fund-raising profession.

I believe the fundamentals will not change.

Here are the 11 factors I believe have governed the work of direct-response fund-raisers for many decades now—and will continue to do so for a great many years to come:

1. Direct response is a *process*, not an event. We use the two-way communications facilities of any direct-response medium to build mutually rewarding relationships with people—donors, members, merchandise buyers, what-have-you. Sustaining this process requires capital investment and patience. Direct-response fund-raising is unlikely ever to become a fast way for a charity to make a buck.

2. The process of direct response gains its true value only over the *long term*. Today, for example, many small-donor direct-mail fund-raising programs are operated by nonprofit organizations that receive only limited financial rewards from the mail itself. The real rewards come over the long haul—often in the form of bequests. That reality is unlikely to change anytime soon.

3. Wise practitioners of direct-response fund-raising keep a sharp eye on their work's *cost-effectiveness*. It's prudent to be much less concerned about costs in their own right. For example, telephone fund-raisers

know today that it's worthwhile to spend more time (and thus invest more money) in calls to higher-dollar donors. Those contacts are more costly but also tend to be more cost-effective. I strongly suspect we'll find it worthwhile to invest more time, effort, and money in our most responsive donors in the future, no matter what else might change.

4. More than any other single factor in direct response today, the *audience* is far and away the most significant. In the case of direct mail and telefund-raising, that's the "list." Other formats—television, radio, and space advertising—speak about the "media buy." It's all the same, though. The hardest-hitting, award-winning appeal won't elicit gifts from the wrong list of people—not today and not tomorrow. Please read Chapter 3 to understand more about future audiences.

5. Assuming the list is well chosen, *the offer* is next in importance in a direct-response appeal. Is it asking for money? How much? What are the benefits to the donor—intangible as well as tangible? These questions, more than any others, tend to determine the response from any given list. If we're not still thinking in terms of "offers" 20 or 30 years from now, I doubt we'll be involved in anything we would choose to call direct response.

6. In appeals to donors, fund-raisers *segment* the list—that is, vary the offer and sometimes other factors as well—because hard experience has proven that it pays to do so. Future technologies may permit fund-raisers to carry the principle of segmentation to a new level—the "individualized" appeals already mentioned—but the principle won't change: Fund-raisers will continue to communicate with different individuals in different ways.

7. No matter how much people believe that their lives are experiencing an accelerating rate of change, one factor remains constant: the *annual calendar*. Humans make our journey from womb to grave at a pace that has remained largely constant for millennia—one year at a time. Today annual giving or membership programs form the backbone of direct-response fund-raisers' relationships with donors. Chances are, such signposts will always be needed to anchor us in time, and the calendar year is the signpost of choice. It doesn't seem likely that the calendar will be fundamentally "reformed" again anytime soon.

8. The measurable results of direct-response communications distinguish them from other forms of advertising, marketing, and (often) fund-raising. Measurements permit fund-raisers to *test*, comparing lists, offers, packages, or other elements, giving rise to incremental improvements in results over time. Fortunately, all the new communications media foreseeable today possess the same central characteristic: Their results can be measured. This suggests that fund-raisers will be testing long after today's time-worn formats and techniques have gone the way of the Selectric II.

9. Like any other form of advertising, direct-response fund-raising requires *repetition* to gain and hold donors' attention. Whether fund-raisers communicate by mail, telephone, television, or radio, they consistently use the same themes, symbols, tag lines, and visual images in a fund-raising campaign to penetrate the fog of competing messages that surround people every day and threaten to muddle even the clearest-thinking mind. If anything, the growing volume of advertising messages and the proliferation of new media may require the use of consistent themes and images even more self-consciously in the decades ahead.

10. A direct-response fund-raising program can flourish without a single letter or a solitary phone call. But whatever medium is used to communicate, there is one indispensable constant: *record keeping.* Surely, an easily accessible database that records donors' behavior over time will be the direct-response fund-raiser's most precious asset 20 years from now, just as it is today.

11. For millennia, stories have defined how people think, the way they learn, and the way they understand their lives. Storytelling has also been integral to direct-response fund-raising. Though some pundits anticipate the end of storytelling with the advent of the new media, I am sure that new technologies will instead redefine narrative. Donors will be able to step into the narrative, interact, and perhaps even change the outcome of a compelling fund-raising story. But no matter what the technology, stories will continue to help organizations and their supporters define, explain, and as understand the world around them.

Conclusion

Will readers be ready for the future, no matter what? With all due respect, I don't think any of us can say that. We just don't know what new surprises and discontinuities life may hold for us in the decades to come. However, if readers of the rest of this book, who ponder the thoughtful discussion the chapters contain about today's cutting-edge direct response technologies and techniques, at least they can say they are familiar with today's fast-evolving state of the art.

But what about all those predictions? Well, we'll see about that. Check back with me around 2020.

Meanwhile, as *Star Trek*'s Mr. Spock always says, "Live long and prosper!"

Making the Case for Direct Response

2

MICHAEL JOHNSTON

Chapter 7 presents a humorous and effective defense of direct-response fund-raising. David Love reminds us that David Ogilvy saw direct response as the last line of defense in advertising, and I have to agree with him—direct response *is* the last line of defense for any organization's fund-raising. Direct response finds fund-raisers' supporters, keeps us in contact with those supporters, and collects their donations. It's the most predictable and calculable medium that can be used to raise money.

Many of the examples in this chapter come from direct-mail fund-raising, but the ideas, issues, tactics, and strategies are relevant to telephone, TV, door-to-door, or Internet direct-response fund-raising as well. This book covers a wide range of mediums—from direct-response television (DRTV) to the telephone to CD-ROMs to the Internet. Please turn to Chapter 5 for an excellent discussion on a new media response strategies and tactics.

Why It Is Important to Have Everyone Committed to Fund-Raising, in Some Capacity

Donors expect more from organizations than every before. They expect excellent communications, their questions answered quickly, to be thanked promptly, and to be asked to events at times. Western societies can be awfully alienating places—with families shrinking in size (does the nuclear family even exist anymore?) and institutions like the church are losing their flock. If Faith Popcorn (a respected futurist) is to be believed, individuals are beginning to "cocoon" behind a wall of entertainment and distractions brought about by covergent technologies like the Internet and television.

If donors expect more, every part of an organization needs to be inculcated with a donor-first perspective—a perspective that places the needs and desires of the donor squarely into forefront of an organization's daily operations. The volunteer who answers the phone, the board member who attends a United Way dinner, the staff person running a program—they all need to be a part of the fund-raising team.

And an essential part of that fund-raising program is direct response.

All actors in a nonprofit organization need to understand and respect direct response. Later in this chapter, we take a look at how one organization has tried to communicate the importance of direct response to its staff and volunteers. The more everyone in an organization understands about direct-response fund-raising, the easier it is for them to answer questions arising from the various fund-raising mediums that an organization uses. Nothing is worse than a volunteer or non–fund-raising staffer communicating ignorance or prejudices to a donor on the phone. A donor may call to complain about his or her name being traded by that organization, and the staff person or volunteer doesn't know how to explain what's happened.

But why educate the staff and volunteers of an organization about the basics of direct-response fund-raising?

First off, direct-response fund-raising is very important. A wide range of nonprofit organizations raise anywhere from 20 to up to 60 percent of their fund-raising budgets from direct response. It is an extremely important source of fund-raising income for hundreds of thousands of nonprofits in the United States.

Many staffers and volunteers don't think they have to learn about media that is going to die. The demise of direct mail (especially) has been predicted for the last 20 years, yet there is more mail being sent out than ever before.

Whither Direct Mail: A Survey

For more ammunition to defend direct-mail fund-raising from those predicting its demise, this study was conducted for the NSFRE International Fund Raising Conference in Dallas in April 1998.

The survey asked 50 U.S. nonprofit organizations with large direct-mail programs and a number of direct-mail consultants where they thought direct-mail fund-raising was headed.

QUESTION 1. Do you believe more money, less money, or about the same will be raised by direct mail five years into the future? Ten years into the future?

5 years	More	91%
	Less	3%
	About the same	6%

10 years	More	77%
	Less	13%
	About the same	16%

QUESTION 2. Do you believe the privacy movement will negatively impact direct-mail fund-raising results?

	Yes	25%
	No	75%

QUESTION 3. Will younger people, when they reach the traditional giving ages, give to charity like former generations have?

	Yes	81%
	No	19%

QUESTION 4. Will younger people give by direct mail?

	Yes	69%
	No	31%

QUESTION 5. Will the electronic media replace direct mail as the medium of choice for donors?

	Yes	37%
	No	63%

If yes, when?

	2 years	0%
	5 years	17%
	10 years	83%

QUESTION 6. What is the greatest problem you face in raising more money by direct mail (top-rated problem to least mentioned)?

PROBLEM

- Increased costs
- Cost to acquire new donors
- Competition
- Availability of lists
- Decreasing returns
- Government regulations
- Donor confidence
- Creative

Direct mail (and direct response) is always going to be around in one form or another, and staff must respect it, understand some of it, and defend it when needed. When direct-response fund-raising is ignored, all areas of fund-raising suffer. If an organization can't keep track of its small gift givers, then how will it know whom to cultivate into larger and larger gifts?

Direct-response fund-raising is every organization's "ear to the ground." Direct-response donors are often the most knowledgable about a nonprofit organization's work and the first to complain about that work. A good direct-response program is attuned to public support and can adapt when public opinion is shifting on a particular issue.

Outreach—Making Others in the Organization Aware of the Mission

Direct-response fund-raising is often, at best, ignored and, at worst, mis-understood by staff and volunteers in a nonprofit organization. The last thing non–fund-raising staff want to do is try to understand why the fund-raising department sends out "junk mail" or makes bothersome telephone calls. What's more, they simply don't like it because they feel the stories are fake and manipulative. When they see letters starting with "Dear Friend," or a particular gift amount circled, or a P.S. added at the end of a letter as evidence of a system that is actively engaged in fooling donors into giving gifts and exploiting their emotions, countless staffers and volunteers complain that their direct-response fund-raising is just "hitting someone's buttons."

Working with Other Areas of the Development Office

It is vital that all areas of fund-raising (including direct-response fund-raising) are coordinated effectively. Donors may give to a special event, through the telephone, through a lottery, and through a direct-mail gift. They need to have a seamless experience with a nonprofit organization. Sadly, often this is not the case. It hurts a direct-response program when a well-crafted, beautiful direct-mail piece tells donors they haven't given to the organization in two years when in fact they bought a table for a special event two months earlier.

A direct-response fund-raising staff person should ask the following eight questions to help ensure their development office is coordinated:

1. Does the central development office coordinate all fund-raising activities through the organization?
2. Is there an up-to-date organizational chart of the development office?
3. Does the organization chart of the development office clearly illus-trate responsibility for each discrete fund-raising activity?

4. Does the organization chart show one person responsible for each discrete fund-raising activity?
5. Does the organization chart show activities in the development office are arranged into logical groupings, allowing excellent synergy?
6. Is the size of the development staff analyzed on a yearly basis in light of fund-raising potential to determine if increases or decreases in staff are necessary?
7. Does every development staff person have a written job description?
8. Is there no overlap in responsibility in development office job descriptions (i.e., two or more people responsible for the same thing)?

A development office that is well coordinated will allow direct-response fund-raising staff to really soar. Direct-response fund-raising can link so many areas of a development office, but it can also run into so many roadblocks. The database focus, predictability, and measurable nature of direct-response fund-raising can help other less predictable forms of fund-raising find more discipline and focus.

Taking Advantage of Synergy between Fund-Raising Media

Every organization, including nonprofit ones, has a database that is made up of many more names than just direct-mail donors. One session at the National Society of Fundraising Executives (NSFRE) International Conference in March of 1996 is particularly relevant to the issue of getting non–direct-mail donors to give through the mail and direct-mail donors to join special events. That session presented some example mailings that reemphasized how well-crafted appeals can get direct-mail donors to join special events and then to give to direct mail.

The secret of profitable cross-fertilization is to craft a personal appeal that talks directly to the supporter (special participant or donor in other ways) and tries to persuade that supporter to give in another manner. An organization should not miss any opportunity to do two things: get more people to participate in events and give a direct donation.

The same NSFRE conference provided excellent examples from the Multiple Sclerosis Society of America, which decided to actively mail cross-stream. By so doing, the society saw a 47 percent rise in dollars raised per donor in 1995. It used a number of strategies:

- An MS walkathon letter that thanked the sponsor for walking in the past (making reference to when and how much they raised through sponsorship) and asked if they could make an extra gift this year—asked them to "go an extra mile."
- An MS package that tried to get direct-mail donors to participate in special events. The exterior teaser said "Official Registration Kit"; and on the back said, "Return this form and get ready for prizes, excitement, and a fun filled event to help MS." There was heavy emphasis on the event in the text of the letter, including a calendar in the middle right of the front page.
- An MS bike-a-thon appeal that showed a graphic of a bike on the front and the teaser "HEY YOU, the one who loves to ride your bike, YES YOU, here's big news about the Ultimate biking experience." The letter began, "Picture the ultimate biking experience . . ." Then the bike-a-thon was described, describing the great time to be had.
- There is every effort to make sure that corporate donor matching gift challenges exist for these cross-stream mailings. The gift array begins "I understand my donation will be matched by X corporation," and the corporate logo appears on the reply coupon and the company's support is explained in the letter's postscript.

These are just some of the cross-stream opportunities that can inspire any organization to do the same. Almost every nonprofit organization can create an effective cross-stream opportunity for direct-mail donors and special event participants and donors.

Corporate supporter lists also need to be contacted in an improved direct-response program. Two mailings a year (year-end and child-focused appeal) are excellent chances to get corporate direct-response money from current donors. In addition, lists can be rented and compiled and new appeals sent out.

There should also be an increase in direct mail directed to planned giving goals. It would make sense in the second or third year of an improved direct-response program to test a mailing to loyal supporters that introduces them to planned giving.

What to Do with Success

As organizations improves their systems in support of their direct-response fund-raising program, often they'll have to deal with the following issues:

- Increased volume of mail to be opened and entered onto properly maintained daily tracking sheets. This will mean extra time spent by a direct-mail assistant.
- Increased volume of work in coordinating print quotes, print production, and lettershop.
- Dealing with the higher volume of donor inquiries. With more information and solicitation packages in the mail, there is more contact from donors, and there needs to be a staff person who understands both the donor and the direct-mail program. (A Web site can help relieve some of the staff pressure.)
- Processing and coordinating the preauthorized payment donors from the direct-response program.
- Creating and sending out the first welcome packages to first-time donors.

As an improved direct-response program draws more responses, nonprofit staff need to gauge the workload from the increased volumes of mail. Temporary help will be able to deal with the first wave of increased responses, but external help may have to be hired to process further increases in the workload.

There needs to be a strong policies and procedures document for the fund-raising staff that can help new personnel understand the direct-response fund-raising program and can assist non–fund-raising staff to comprehend the complementary role they can play in direct-response fund-raising. That document will outline what should be done when someone calls to complain about a direct-mail package, who speaks with that person, and if any follow-up letter is necessary.

COMPLAINT FORM

Name of Donor	Address, Phone	Donation History	Programs and Issues Highlighted	Comments	Follow-Up

The policies and procedures document for direct-response fund-raising should also include an explanation of list trading, an explanation of why more packages are sent out, and an explanation of why packages are crafted as they are. Their formats have been effective in raising money for the organization.

The material should provide much of the expert background needed to explain the expanded direct-response fund-raising program to other staff and volunteers.

There also needs to be a consistent form that can add information over the years about a direct-response donor's special needs. There should be a binder (which some organizations call a "tickler binder")—an informal contact management document to keep track of sensitive direct-mail donor/supporter needs. This binder needs to be widely understood within the organization and key staff need to know about it. For example, perhaps a $2,000-a-year direct-mail donor only wants a solicitation in December through the mail and likes a call about the summer camp program in May. The person doesn't want any other correspondence. He also was a past board member, and he likes anyone on the phone to make reference to that past relationship. These facts should be entered into the tickler binder, which stands outside the database and includes details of conversations held with sensitive donors.

Proper Clerical Support

To ensure that fund-raising staff can take full advantage of direct-response fund-raising techniques and strategies, there needs to be the proper clerical support. Even if nonprofit managers were to read through this book and understand what techniques and strategies they need to implement, their campaigns will grind to a halt without clerical staff.

Fund-raising staff need to be freed up from many clerical duties so they can concentrate and exercise their knowledge. Doctors have clerical staff to take paperwork away from them. They are able to practice their profession. It must be the same for direct-response fund-raising staff.

What follows are a series of 10 questions that every direct-response fund-raising staff person needs to ask to ensure a proper clerical support environment.

1. Are professional fund-raising staff not performing functions in the fund-raising office that should instead be performed by clerical staff?
2. Are clerical positions documented with written instructions?
3. Are clerical employees in the fund-raising office asked to complete a formal training program when hired?
4. Is clerical support sufficient to meet the fund-raising office workload?

5. Do clerical employees in the fund-raising office present themselves in person and on the telephone in a personable and pleasant manner?
6. Are the sequence of steps in direct-response fund-raising procedures the best possible and clearly outlined and understood?
7. Do clerical staff use tools like Microsoft's Project 2000 to help direct-response fund-raising staff to control their projects?
8. Are the direct-response fund-raising forms (for production and tracking, e.g.), reviewed every year as to their usefulness and ease of handling?
9. Is the telephone answering system adequate for receiving messages?
10. Is fund-raising correspondence from the fund-raising office prepared and edited in a professional manner?

With the proper clerical support, direct-response fund-raisers will be able to excel at their professional work.

Volunteers

Many nonprofit organizations do a good job of integrating volunteers into fund-raising, but a special effort should be made to get them more involved in direct-response fund-raising volunteering—especially as it relates to getting volunteers to improve the relationship with donors. The challenge will be finding them work that has some value to themselves and the donor they interact with.

Progress Without People?
The Case Study of a Direct-Response Volunteer

Bernice Irish is a 74-year-old past volunteer fund-raising leader for The March of Dimes of Ontario. She worked for 30 years as a volunteer direct-response fund-raiser. She stuffed envelopes and was sent a stipend that allowed her to pay for the postage for an unaddressed mail drop in her community—the town of Simcoe, population 15,000.

She would call the post office every year and ask for the number of residential addresses in the town and then order that exact quantity of direct mail packages from the central office in Toronto. The package didn't change for decades: a letter, reply coupon, and return envelope addressed to her home.

The letter would tell a story set in the nearby city of Toronto. Bernice would field occasional complaints from citizens. Her year-to-year results did not go up over the decades, and she usually got around 200 responses mailed back to her each year. She thought this was a poor result—but in actual fact it is a wonderful result if you have the bigger picture in mind for direct-mail fund-raising. But she wasn't given the bigger picture and was given no goals to meet or break.

When the mail came back to her, she'd create her yearly ledger of donors and issue receipts to the generous, loyal supporters of The March of Dimes. The end came in 1989, when she handed control of the direct-mail program to the central office in Toronto. She sent in the ledgers, which were a meticulous record of decades of giving in her community.

To be honest, she was happy to hand it over. She and about 10 local volunteers were getting older, and it was getting harder to do it year after year. She was told that Toronto would pick up the cultivation of these supporters in the future.

Without responsibility for direct-mail fund-raising or any other task, the volunteers drifted away. Bernice wished that some kind of connection to the local donors could have been kept. Perhaps the volunteers could have been given responsibility for calling or visiting local donors after a gift had been made through the mail. Bernice would have loved going to a tea and to have a quick chat with donors she knew quite well.

As a church leader for decades, Bernice knows that personal contact cultivates generous supporters, and she was sad to see The March of Dimes lose that personal contact with the hundreds of its supporters in the town.

Are nonprofit organizations losing the wonderful human resources left over from past direct-response fund-raising methods while adopting new ones? The nonprofit sector should follow trends that lead to progress with people—not without them. That will lead to more profitable fund-raising in the long term.

An improved computer system theoretically can handle the increased demands of the increased direct-response volume. (See Chapter 4 for more on computerized database issues). Every nonprofit needs to ensure that its database can provide fast, accurate gift processing, and complete and accurate data entry that includes: name and address, preferred title, full current address, date, source, and amount of first gift and of subsequent gifts and name of spouse.

Direct-response fund-raising continues to be a counterintuitive medium that demands training for staff to best understand and execute a direct-mail program. There needs to be more professional development opportunities for fund-raising staff and volunteers in a fast-moving direct-response fund-raising environment. Resources must be allocated for books, magazines, newsletters, and conferences that can help give staff the most up-to-date skills for direct-response fund-raising.

And once the materials are on-site, a formal system of passing on fund-raising magazines and subscription materials between staff must be established. Sharing with other nonprofit organizations should be formalized if possible. Any direct-response fund-raising program is vital to the long-term survival of a nonprofit organization. That vital role necessitates professional development to make sure direct-response returns continue to grow.

No organization can afford to keep fund-raising endeavors away from one another. For example, it's been traditional for special events to keep a good distance from direct-response fund-raising. In the new direct-response fund-raising environment, this should no longer happen.

Working with Organization Staff

Staff and volunteers in nonprofit organizations outside of the fund-raising department often are not supportive of their own direct-mail fund-raising. (The same problem can arise within a fund-raising department.)

Often they think it's all junk mail. (See chapter appendix.) They may not understand how and why they could help the fund-raising department find supporters to tell powerful fund-raising stories.

A number of strategies can help the fund-raising department both explain its work and tell better stories. Staff members can begin by creating campaign thermometers, updates, sample packages, and comment pages in a public place within the organization's offices. They also can ask staff and volunteers to compile an up-to-date list of good fund-raising stories for the department. Furthermore, they may use staff, volunteers, and students to interview and compile stories for the fund-raising copywriter.

In addition, the organization needs to make sure the storytellers are thanked and must ensure word gets around that sharing stories with the nonprofit organization is valuable. Finally, with a commitment to conduct more involved interviews, the fund-raising copywriter needs to use effective interview techniques that capture all of the vital fund-raising elements in someone's story.

By following the following (four) rules, staff and volunteers will learn to love direct-mail fund-raising—or, at the least, to think of direct mail as a vital and honest part of the organization's external communications, relationship-building, and fund-raising.

1. Show me
2. Inventory the stories
3. Treat storytellers with a caring touch
4. Got its best from someone's story

1. Show Me

Perhaps the main reason direct-response fund-raising is so misunderstood in nonprofit organizations is that campaigns often exist outside the view of staff and volunteers. The only time they get a chance to see a direct-mail package is when an irate board member or neighbor waves a package in front of their face, loudly complaining about its manipulative style and how the organization must be wasting money with a four page letter.

Increase understanding of the direct-response campaigns by creating a campaign update area outside the fund-raising offices, perhaps in the cafeteria or some other public place. Begin by creating a number of direct-mail campaign "thermometers," like the one seen in Exhibit 2.1. Before each solicitation goes into the mail, put up a thermometer with the name of the campaign and the dollar goal. As the money comes in, fill up the thermometer to the amount of money that has been donated. Staff and volunteers can come by and see how the package is performing. A staff member might walk by, see the package is not going to make its goal, and know why. Perhaps the person thought there was a more riveting story that could have been told and knows who should be interviewed for the next package on that subject.

Outside the office, put up a sample box. Put a number of samples in the box when a new package goes into the mail. The outside of the box tells a passersby to "Take a sample and see what's in the mail right now." Include a comment page in each sample. Ask staff and volunteers to look at the package, see how the campaign is performing on the thermometer, and provide comments on what's good and bad about the package. How could it be better next time?

A fund-raising department might also think of posting interesting and inspiring responses from donors. I can remember looking through responses from donors that helped craft future fund-raising packages. I especially remember one response from a donor to a health charity. The donor, in response to a research-focused solicitation, wanted to tell the organization that blueberries were a sure-fire way to cure this devastating disease. The letter for future research solicitation could begin by recounting this folk cure. The letter could then reiterate how wonderful it would

EXHIBIT 2.1   United Nations Association—Direct-Response Result Thermometer

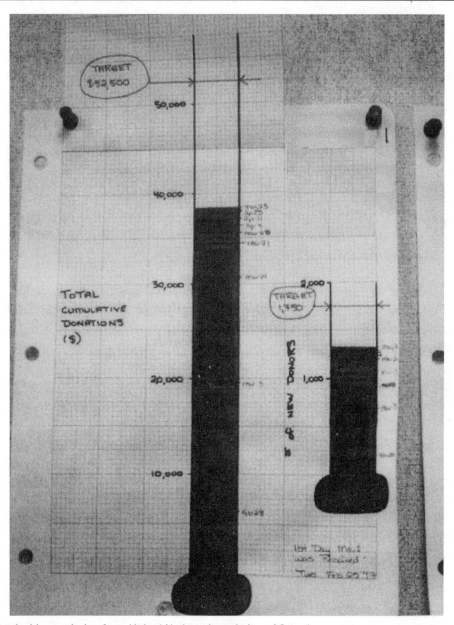

Used with permission from United Nations Association of Canada.

be if blueberries could end this disease, but how it also showed how desperate people were for a cure and how the donor should help find a real answer to the disease.

By posting thanks, comments, and stories from donors, staff and volunteers can see how seriously the public takes the direct-mail fund-raising packages that arrive in their mailboxes. Of course, be sure to black out the name and address of the letter writer in any letters posted in a hallway or public place.

Show Me the Money:
How One Organization Posts Its Direct Response Results

The United Nations Association of Canada (UNAC) implemented a strategy to publicly exhibit elements of its direct-response fund-raising program. Lynn Broughton, donor liaison for the UNAC, feels their public exhibits (which include thermometers and mail summaries) "generate interest and understanding of the direct response program."

Further, Broughton outlines how "staff and volunteers will sometimes come to me with an idea for a future direct mail campaign. Before the public displays (which started about two years ago) there'd be less input on the content of the direct mail appeals. Now staff and volunteers are more comfortable with what we're doing in the fund-raising department and aren't afraid to approach us with an idea. We have a once-a-month meeting where staff have a chance to comment on the fund-raising campaigns. Since putting up the displays their comments are more astute and helpful."

Broughton goes on to say that "Board members gravitate to the displays to see how our campaigns are doing. For me the public display area lets people find out more about our direct response without knocking on my door and interrupting my work. For staff and volunteers, they are using the displays to help them know how our funding base is doing. Many nonprofit organizations are fragile. They need successful fund-raising programs to continue to carry out their mission. Our displays have become a symbol of stability. And if they weren't doing well, then we'd probably get more educated comments and help from staff and volunteers who now understand more about the importance of this program to the strength of the organization."

2. Inventory of the Stories

Real life is always more riveting, heartfelt, and effective than fiction. That's especially true in direct-mail fund-raising. Listening to a real-life story of someone who's received a heart transplant or won a fight against cancer makes for the best kind of fund-raising copy. When organizations turn to composite stories, with a fictionalized name, the story is often missing a complexity and emotional weight that longer, more involved stories can provide. However, often direct-mail fund-raising practitioners don't have access to the best stories. A nonprofit organization may help many citizens, but they haven't made a commitment to catalog those whom they've helped and who would make excellent interview candidates.

The Heart and Stroke Foundation of Manitoba has made such a list, for a number of purposes. It's a resource for the communications department, but it is also a great resource for creating effective copy for the direct-mail fund-raising campaign. Any organization can make a similar document. Simply follow the following outline: the document should provide the name, address, and telephone numbers of individuals with a story to tell—each of them categorized under separate program areas. Under each name there is additional information about how they've provided information in past campaigns and other communications initiatives (e.g., newsletter stories, articles, etc.). From this list, a direct-mail copywriter can find the proper story for a particular solicitation. What's more, the Heart and Stroke Foundation of Manitoba makes sure that individuals who call their 1-800 help line, and have stirring and important stories to tell, are put on a database and the information is passed on to the communications and fund-raising departments. Many of the fund-raising stories for the organization come from these callers. Other nonprofit organizations should think of ways to funnel stories from where stories are gathered—whether that's through a 1-800 number, support groups, or other programs and services—to the fund-raising department. Of course, individuals would be contacted first before any stories would be told to the public. Confidentiality is the priority; fund-raising, second.

Nonprofit staff are often overly protective of individuals who've been helped through their organization. They often tell the direct-mail copywriter that they shouldn't approach the person because the story is too personal—too sensitive. In over 10-years of interviewing individuals in order to translate their stories into direct-mail fund-raising solicitations, I've never had someone say no. Furthermore, I've never had anyone ask me to use a pseudonym.

One young man who had been diagnosed with a form of arthritis hadn't even told his boss yet. He thought if he told the boss, he might lose his job.

That very fact became the letter's postscripts: "P.S. I haven't even told my boss about my osteoarthritis yet, but I'm taking a chance and telling you about it today because it's vital you understand why you need to renew your support for The Arthritis Society."

He was willing to tell others about his arthritis and how the Arthritis Society helped him and ask readers to support the organization, but he still couldn't tell his boss. Though he realized that his boss might read this letter, he still wanted to tell his story. Perhaps he thought this was his best chance to explain how his arthritis didn't prevent him from performing his duties at work.

The Canadian Diabetes Association of Manitoba took their list of stories to another level. They used a summer student to contact a wide range of volunteers and clients and interview them. The stories were 250 to 1000 words long, and provided the direct-mail copywriter with useful material. Val Bingeman, the direct-response coordinator at the time; explains: "We did it because we wanted to have a bank of stories to use in local media that were representative of local towns. We wanted authentic stories that showed the work of the Canadian Diabetes Association. It also became an effective source of direct-mail fund-raising stories. We didn't want a situation where we used composite stories. Authenticity always raises more money in our experience."

3. Treat Storytellers with a Caring Touch

When people have helped a nonprofit organization by sharing their stories with supporters, the organization must recognize that intimate contribution. The Arthritis Society of Alberta did just that with the man just described.

The Arthritis Society made sure they thanked their storyteller. They invited him to their office on his lunch hour. The storyteller was presented with a pile of gifts: a sweat shirt, a pen, pin, and mug. In addition, they gave him a thank-you card. Nonprofit organizations need to treat the individuals who are willing to share their stories with thousands of strangers in this way. Carmen Wyton, the regional manager of the Arthritis Society's Edmonton office, states, "It is important to recognize a person's story given to a fund-raising campaign. It's not always easy to share something so personal. We need to tell that person that their gift of a story is incredibly important and valued by the organization."

It was a special moment for the young man with arthritis, the organization, the staff, and the direct-mail program.

4. Get the Best from Someone's Story

Once the right person has been chosen to interview, a copywriter has to make sure to get the best story out of the interviewee. I've never created a fund-raising line, word, or sentence that is as powerful as something a person has told me.

Remember the following points when conducting a direct-response fund-raising interview:

- Listen more than you talk. Have a glass of water nearby, and make sure that you sip that water as you listen. It'll keep you quiet.
- Be patient. Don't be afraid to let interviewees ramble. Try not to set a predetermined time for the interview. Say it'll only take a short amount of time, but then sit back and let it go as long as people wants it to. Sometimes a person will be heading down a narrative you think won't yield the emotional gold that you're mining for. Suddenly—wham—he'll tell you something that'll make your fund-raising antennae tingle and stand on end.
- If you're interviewing young people, try to use words they're comfortable with. For example, ask them what they think is cool about summer camp. Don't ask them what the camp means to them.
- Ask them how they were first introduced to the nonprofit organization.
- Ask them about their family and friends, and what they've meant to them in comparison to the nonprofit organization. Don't put it in terms of comparisons, but asking them about family and friends will provide a more emotional, honest, and compelling story.
- After hearing about family, ask how they were introduced to the nonprofit and what the organization has done to help them. Ask them where they would be if the nonprofit organization didn't exist. This often provides a powerful reason for the donor to make a donation.
- Explain to interviewees that their story will be sent to X thousand people, and this is their best chance to say what they'd like to the public. If they had one thing to say to these people, what would it be? Remind them how these folks are past supporters and they'll be asked to give again.
- Always be aware of an inanimate object that could be a powerful icon in the story. Film director Alfred Hitchcock called this object the McGuffin: the all-important object whose pursuit frames a narrative,

like the Maltese Falcon or the uranium-packed wine bottles in his movie *Notorious*. A fund-raiser should look for the McGuffin in a direct-mail fund-raising story. You can call it the Mc*Gift*en, the all-important object that frames a fundraising story.

Following are two stories of uncovering a McGuffin or Mc*Gift*en. In researching a year-end package for a homeless shelter in Toronto, I listened to the story of a recent immigrant who had gotten into trouble with the law. He couldn't get his house key to his wife. He told shelter staff that he was the breadwinner in the house, and without him, he didn't know how she'd survive. The shelter staff delivered both food and the key to the woman. I immediately focused on the key. We took a paper rubbing of a key and included it in the letter. (See Exhibit 2.2.)

In the second case, I was interviewing a longtime volunteer with the Arthritis Society. After 30 minutes of a phone interview, she mentioned a foam tip she'd received from the organization. She explained how the foam tip went on the end of a pen or pencil, mading it easier to grip and use. She

---

EXHIBIT 2.2   Tell a Powerful Story

went on to explain how she'd been the family communicator, sending letters to everyone, but when she got arthritis she couldn't fulfill that role any more—until she got the foam tip from the Arthritis Society. We made sure every donor got one of these foam tips in a direct-mail package.

A Direct Response Program Doesn't Have to Be Large or Small—It Needs Only Be Masterfully Executed

It's hard to understand why the nonprofit sector follows direct-mail trends that are relevant only to large fund-raising programs, not to smaller programs. It's an unfortunate case of a fascination with gigantism that leaves out the valuable experiences of small direct-mail programs.

No doubt, there's a lot to learn from direct-mail programs with massive databases, low costs per package because of large print runs, and sophisticated use of laser personalization. While the experiences of some larger nonprofits may be applied to smaller organizations, many larger nonprofit organizations fall prey to what I like to call the Napoleonic syndrome of direct-mail, direct-response fund-raising—they're efficiently organized campaigns with large numbers of pieces ready to fall upon an unsuspecting nation supported by a style that's sometimes distant and imperial.

We don't want to emulate this trend of an emotional distance from the donor—especially if younger age subsets (including Baby Boomers) are more cynical and wary of mass fund-raising appeals in comparison to the Depression and World War II babies (those born from the 1920s through 1945 and outlined in Chapter 3).

Nonprofit organizations don't need to sacrifice the positive aspects of small mailings in their direct-mail programs. What direct-mail practitioners need is some inspiration to revitalize their programs, big or small, especially when it comes to inspiring the Depression and World War II Babies. And who knows, even some Boomers, Busters, and Boomlets might feel inspired enough to jump on board the emotional bandwagon of fund-raising.

To provide that inspiration, I want to tell you the story of three successful mailings that prove small is not only beautiful but also very profitable when it comes to good direct mail. The lessons in these three stories are applicable for any size nonprofit and most appropriate for nonprofits that have gotten a little lost in that Napoleonic style (or trend) of direct-mail fund-raising.

Who Knew We Had a Roger Tory Peterson under Our Noses?

The Sunshine Centres for Seniors—a Toronto, Ontario, charity that provides year-round recreational programs for 1,500 isolated seniors, doesn't have a formal direct mail program and only mails once or twice a year to tell their most loyal supporters (board, ex-board, ex-staff, longtime volunteers) what they're doing.

What could we put in direct mail that no one else could?

Stephanie, a staff member, told me that she had to leave our meeting to supervise an arts and crafts class. I had to ask, "What do they make in class?" She told me that they were working on watercolor paintings of their favorite birds. I went and took a look. The paintings were beautiful and I told Stephanie she had a whole room of great naturalist painters in the tradition of the American Roger Tory Peterson.

We took the ten best paintings and made color photocopies for our mailing. We mailed 221 friends of the organization. Of these, 103 people (47 percent response) sent in a total of $4,900. Sunshine Centres spent $250 on the mailing.

Some respondents called Sunshine Centers and told Stephanie that they were thrilled to receive paintings by people they knew. Each of the 10 paintings we sent out had the artist's name on the bottom. (see Exhibit 2.3.) Almost all of the direct-mail recipients knew the artists personally. It made for a very powerful appeal.

I Feel Like I'm at Camp Again

The WoodGreen Community Centre provides a wide variety of programs for youth, adults, and seniors in southeast Toronto.

It had sent out direct-mail packages in the past, but they had been merely break-even propositions. I was sitting down with their development director as she wondered how to get people to give to the summer camp program for neighborhood kids.

I asked if they had any pictures of the kids having a wonderful time at camp. The development director wasn't sure. They dug around for a day or two and told me that a volunteer had taken some pictures of the kids at camp the year before. The pictures were of professional quality. What an internal resource! We made sure a picture of a happy camper appeared on the exterior envelope and on the letterhead. Now prospective donors could see the kids they were sending to camp.

EXHIBIT 2.3   Sunshine Centre for Seniors Holiday Appeal 1994

Used with permission from Sunshine Centre for Seniors.

Then I asked if the campers wore anything special as WoodGreen Camper kids. The camp program coordinator explained that all children wear a button they make themselves. Each boy or girl draws a picture of something fun, writes their name, and then WoodGreen presses the drawing into a button. Well, that's exactly what we did for each direct-mail recipient. We decided to mail the 100 best friends of the organization (volunteers and unsolicited past donors). Each friend received a camper's pin (a colorful picture and their name drawn by a neighborhood child who wants to go to camp).

The WoodGreen mailing got 54 responses for a total of $2,200. The mailing cost $100 (using leftover letterheads and envelopes). WoodGreen Community Center had found its competitive advantage by discovering free internal resources—the professional photo and beautiful, personalized pins drawn by neighborhood kids. No other organization could talk to donors about their neighborhood as intimately as WoodGreen. That's why this package proved the adage "Small is beautiful."

That's One Ugly Package!

The Canadian Diabetes Association (CDA) of Manitoba, Canada, provides programs and projects that help all Manitobans, young and old, dealing with diabetes. The program was quite a bit bigger than that the other organizations discussed. It had 15,000 donors who had given in the last year and a total database of 80,000 lapsed donors and contact names.

We had to mail to CDA supporters about their summer camp program. Kids went to beautiful lakeside cabins and adventured their way to greater independence and control of their own diabetes. We didn't really have a budget for the mailing, so what could we do?

First, I decided it was time to find some paper stock that no one wanted—something that was accumulating dust in some printer's warehouse. We found it—some ugly deep-orange envelopes and letterhead that looked like Halloween rejects. The printer would give it to us for next to nothing, just to clean out one corner of his warehouse.

Now that we had started on the homely look, we took it a step further and decided that a rough-drawn camp logo and CDA address could appear as a peel-off sticker in the top left of the envelope. Similarly, the name and address would appear as a contrasting white sticker. (See Exhibit 2.4.)

The effect was shockingly effective and virtually free of cost. Of course, the letter told a good story. Approximately 800 donors were mailed who had either sent their children to camp, or had told us they

EXHIBIT 2.4   Canadian Diabetes Association—Manitoba Division: Camp Appeal

CAMP BIRCHBARK
283 Portage Ave. - 2nd Floor
Winnipeg, MB. R3B 2B5

Bang!
Crash!
Grunt!
Yeah!

Jane Sample
123 Lane
Winnipeg, MB
R0X 0AZ

Used with permission from Canadian Diabetes Association—Manitoba Division.

thought the camp program was important. Those 800 donors were presented with the shocking orange cast-off package and gave a very generous $15,000. CDA spent approximately $500 on the mailing.

It's unfortunate that large programs often dictate trends in direct-mail fund-raising. There's too much written about how to maintain huge databases and how to get the most out of more and more sophisticated laser personalization. We need to step back from the Napoleonic syndrome in direct mail that sacrifices the personal for supposed efficiency. Instead, we need to look at some of the values behind small direct-mail packages, such as the ones just outlined.

The Sunshine Centre's use of arts and crafts class paintings and Wood-Green Community Centre's camper pin are good examples of how the most effective gifts and premiums are often items coming out of our own internal programs and projects. A donor surely wants a one-of-a-kind gift more than a Hallmark card.

The WoodGreen Community Centre's kid's photo should remind us that you don't always have to buy professional or stock photos or resources to make your direct-mail package persuasive.

And finally, the Canadian Diabetes Association's ugly orange envelopes and letterhead show that the resourcefulness of looking to see what printed material others don't appreciate can give you lower production costs and make your packages unlike any other that arrives in a donor's mailbox.

If we remember that small can be beautiful—and profitable in direct mail—then maybe we'll keep more donors involved and committed (especially Depression and World War II babies, but maybe even more Boomers, Busters, and Boomlets) through direct-mail programs (and any direct-response program), large or small.

Conclusion

Direct response fund-raising is essential to any fund-raising program. It is the only medium that allows an organization to have an evolving relationship with a large number of supporters. In addition, it is the medium most affected by new technologies (the Internet and improved databases), and technologies that provide more tools to take care of and nuture more donors than ever.

But because staff and volunteers often hold direct-response fund-raising in disdain, it's benefits must be emphasized.

Making the case for direct-response fund-raising demands a far-reaching strategy that includes three things:

1. Ensuring staff and volunteers understand and respect direct-response fund-raising
2. Making sure that the development office has the policies and procedures in place for staffing, development staff coordination, and proper software and hardware set up
3. Mastering new techniques, creative methods, and technologies to prove to staff, volunteers, and board members that you are a direct-response practitioner they should put their trust in.

APPENDIX A: *Survey Results from the Heart and Stroke Foundation of Manitoba*

The Heart and Stroke Foundation of Manitoba made a commitment to improving nondevelopment staff's understanding of direct-response fund-raising, especially direct-mail fund-raising. The following results come from a series of questions sent to staff. Once these results were compiled, a two-day curriculum was crafted that focused on their comments, doubts and fears.

Out of that session came a stronger respect for the work of the direct-response team from other staff and management. Look at the results to help you understand what your nondevelopment staff (and volunteers) may think of direct-response fund-raising. These answers will help you anticipate the problems that will arise within your organization and indicate how you can prepare answers for their questions and complaints.

If you've ever wanted to climb inside the heads of other staff, here's your chance. Remain calm.

1. **How do you define direct mail? What is it?**
   - Mail sent to past supporters
   - Sent to a specific person or organization calling for action
   - Letter of introduction and request
   - Lots of logistics
   - Need letter, target mailing list, attractive product, incentives and powerful messages
   - Addressed or unaddressed
   - Mass mail to individuals and businesses in our database
   - Rented or traded mailing lists
   - Querying for names in database
   - Merging names
   - Stuffing envelopes
   - Sending it by bulk mail
   - Send donation brochure to someone's house

2. **What activities are involved?**
   - Access audience, implement campaign, evaluate program
   - Market research, creative communications/letter writing, data mining, mailing logistics
   - Send out mail and then follow-up with some type of follow-up, be it phone, or another letter, etc.

- Persuade the individual to give and then, once captured, maintain a mutually beneficial relationship, educating your donor in the process

3. What's the goal in a direct-mail campaign?
- Get as many people as possible to respond or to act
- Get as many people as possible to look at it
- Defined by number of letters sent out, but estimate $2 per letter is achievable
- To get donations from areas where you're unable to get a door-to-door program established
- Ask for money or sell product then tell: inform and educate
- To make lots of money without having to spend a lot
- To meet or exceed yearly $ goal
- Tap (contact) a very large volume of people with a success rate good enough to meet your financial goals

4. Do you like direct mail?
- Is this question a personal or professional one?
- I like direct mail that is local, honest, and realistic and pulls on my heart strings.
- Generally, I don't mind direct mail because it can eliminate some of the junk mail.
- I don't like direct mail when the offer is questionable—i.e., lotteries where your odds aren't very good.
- I think it's all right because addressed to one person.
- I don't usually read direct mail pieces.
- Yes and no. It can be good but can cause a loss of revenue for door to door.
- Yes, because it's a proven marketing tool.
- I enjoy direct mail.
- I will only read it if the letter is short.
- Personally, I do not like direct mail. I'd rather give to someone at the door.
- I feel guilty when I receive direct mail and then don't choose them as one of the charities I'll support that year.
- No. I do not read any direct mail I'm currently receiving. I view them as wasted paper and time.
- I like it when they have a personal appeal and you can clearly see why they would benefit from my donation.

- Sometimes. Some mailings are very pushy, others awfully sappy, and some just don't hit home.
- Yes and no. The letters are typically too long.
- No. I resent the assumption that since I've given in the past that I'll continue to do so in the future.

YES	AMBIGUOUS	NO
4	7	5

5. **Describe some of your experiences with fund-raising direct-mail packages, especially with other health-related charities.**
- Other direct-mail packages that I like are ones that give something back to me or the community. The package should be bright, color-ful, and have an interesting look to it.
- I deal with two religious charities who both mail me. They usually enclose a small gift (a card or address labels seem to be popular) with their request.
- I scan them to see what's different about the piece compared to ours. I have read two complete direct-mail pieces in the last eight years.
- Like to know what's asked for upfront, no hidden agenda.
- Direct-mail letters usually end up in the recycle bin before they are opened—unless I am "tricked" into opening it by a deceiving envelope and I don't know what it is.
- I get most of my direct mail from humane societies. They send me address labels (love them!), calendars (nice!), and Christmas cards (handy) and I send them money about 25 percent of the time.
- The Salvation Army has recently impressed me with their mail campaign.
- Personally I find that I don't even take the time to open direct mail because in my experience it is all a plea for donations. My overall experience with direct-mail fund-raising is negative. I also am left with the impression that the fund-raising organization is attempting to take "the easy way out"—garnering dollars in a cheap fashion.

6. **Whom do you give to through the mail and why? Are there other methods of fund-raising that you prefer to give through?**
- I don't give very often (if ever at all) through the mail. Most of my donations are given to door-to-door campaigners or to organiza-tions I'm directly involved with. It's harder to say no to someone at the door.

- I give to organizations within the Roman Catholic Church. I even got a letter from a mission in Durban, South Africa, which incuded a small religious token. I do notice I get more letters once I've given. I find that a little irritating but I believe in the cause anyway.
- I don't give through the mail. Employee deduction giving is more efficient.
- I don't give through the mail anymore because I gave once and they then kept sending me donation brochures every four months. It almost became a nuisance. I like to give once a year.
- I give to no one through the mail.
- Yes. I support charities who do work in our province. I like to keep my dollars here.
- I give mostly to humane societies through the mail. I am a huge animal lover/owner and very soft-hearted toward them. I don't like it when they send me pictures of the cruelty to animals, but understand the possible benefits in other cases.
- I do not give through the mail. I am on so many phone lists I do not donate and become a target for more charities. I prefer payroll deduction.
- I don't give through the mail. I like to be able to give at the door. I am cautious giving over the phone or through the mail to charities I don't know much about.
- I don't give through the mail. I have identified charities I prefer to support and give to them regularly.
- I prefer to give face to face. I also prefer to give service, not just money.
- I choose a few that are related to my family's needs.
- I don't currently give through the mail. I understand that for a lot of people who give through direct mail—ease of giving is the issue. You write a check and send it out—no fuss/no muss. For me, the workplace salary deducation achieves ease of giving.

NO	YES
10	4

APPENDIX B: An Examination and Explanation of the Three Year Plan

It's often difficult to plan a direct response program visually. You know what you have to do over the next three years, but sometimes it's hard to show other staff members or board members what you are trying to accomplish.

A color-coded, simple-to-use, three-year scheduling document is included at the end of this chapter and on the accompanying CD-ROM. Every direct-response practitioner should use this schedule to explain the program to staff and board. You can project the file up on a screen through the lens of an overhead or an LCD projector.

The three years outlined at the end of Appendix B represent the direct-mail program for the Heart and Stroke Foundation of Manitoba. Special events, telephone fund-raising, prospecting, monthly donor programs, and the like are all referenced within the schedule. In addition, the plans list page numbers. These visual references were coordinated with a supporting text document that explained, clearly and succinctly, why each of these strategies and tactics was being used for this organization.

The more other staff understand what is done in direct-response fund-raising, the more respect the fund-raising program will get.

How the Plan Helps You Stick to the Schedule

This direct-response map will help you plan the frequency of renewal mailings in the context of the organization's strategic direction. By following this kind of schedule, you'll get out more mail, and if it is targeted to the right audiences, it should make you a higher net profit.

The plan will remind you to plan, test, and execute:

1. An annual cycle
2. Monthly giving
3. Corporate and special events tied into the direct-response programs
4. Renewal cycles
5. Specials
6. Welcome packages
7. Direct-response TV, telephone

8. Upgrades
9. Story banks
10. Premiums
11. Proper tracking of results
12. Professional development for staff

Year 1999   Reinvigorated Direct Response Program

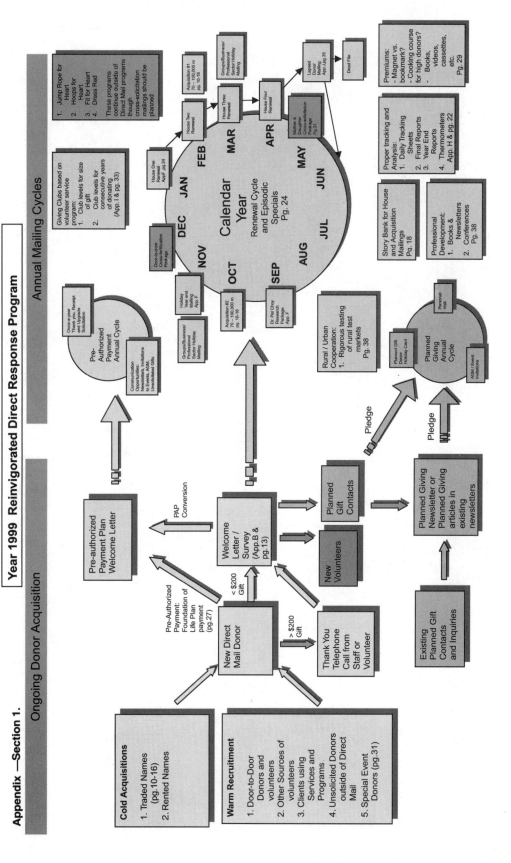

Year 2000 Reinvigorated Direct Response Program

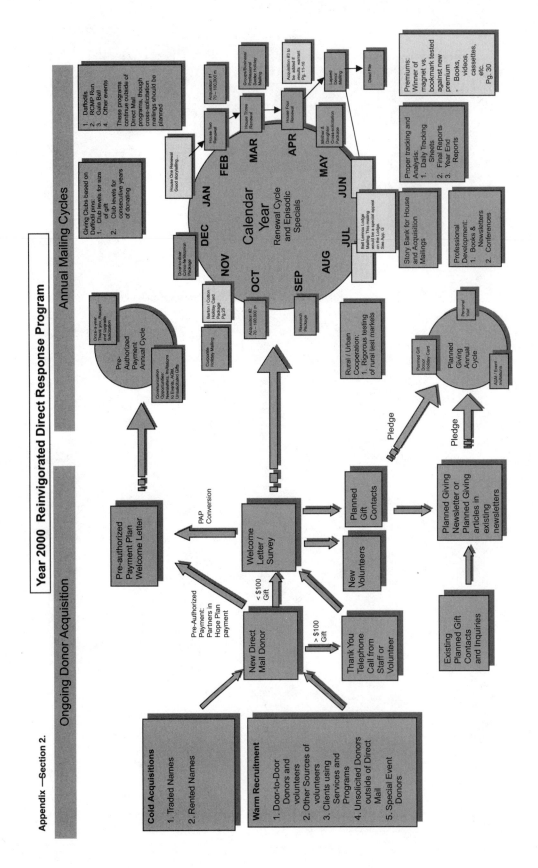

Year 2001 Reinvigorated Direct Response Program

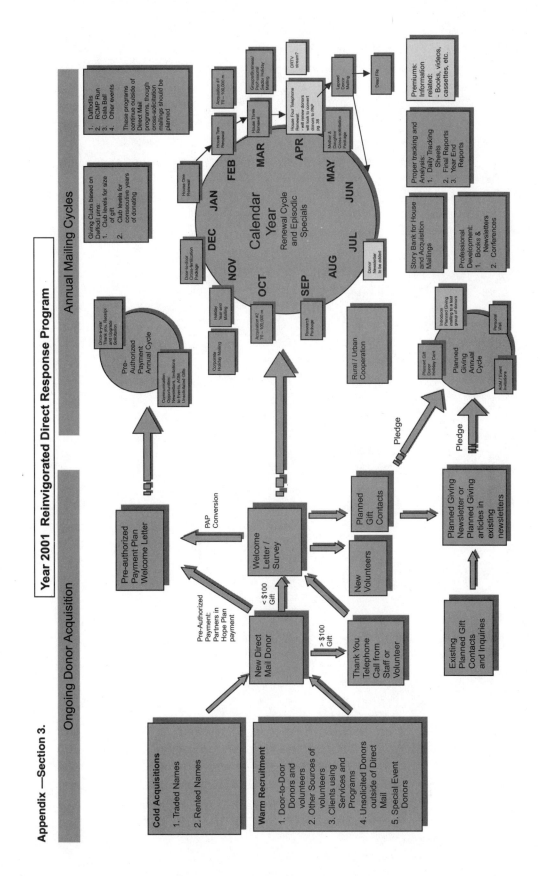

New Audiences with Direct-Response Fund-Raising

Judith E. Nichols

While fund-raisers delight in trading stories about the "once-in-a-lifetime" major gifts they have secured, most development officers know that consistent, modest annual gifts—usually solicited through the mail, phone, or door-to-door campaigns—ensure the health of their organizations and provide the current unrestricted dollars so necessary for essential day-to-day operations. These modest gifts also pave the way for major and planned giving.

However, something essential has changed in direct-response fund-raising: the audiences. Since people are living longer, we now have several adult generations—each with its own unique set of marketing vulnerabilities. This chapter will help any direct-response professional understand, choose, and execute the right strategies (right mediums) for each package (subset) now and in the near future.

What Separates the Generations?

Rebecca Piirto, in *Beyond Mind Games: The Marketing Power of Psychographics*, describes a study by DuPont and Management Horizons that focused on shared experiences. It starts with the assumption that people are shaped by the events they experience during youth: "People of the same age tend to behave in similar ways because they went through the same formative experiences. During the formative years—between the ages of 7 and 21—core values and attitudes are shaped that will affect an individual for life."

As people mature, other influences take over, such as college, marriage, pursuing a career, and/or raising a family. Overriding all of these personal influences are the broader events—political, social, international, technological, and economic—that shape all of our lives. As a result, we have different points of reference and individually unique childhood experiences.

To understand the differences between generations, we need to ask how people were raised as children, what public events they witnessed in adolescence, and what social mission elders gave them as they came of age.

Each generation has its own personality. Projecting generational personality/activity is a new way of predicting consumer attitudes and lifestyles. Historians William Strauss and Neil Howe, in their book *Generations: The History of America's Future, 1584 to 2069*, suggest we can read behavior along a "generational diagonal." According to the authors, there are four "generational personalities"—idealistic, reactive, civic, and adaptive—that recur in that order throughout history. To succeed in reaching the generations, fund-raising messages will have to pay attention not only to where a generation has been but to where it is headed. (The terms "cohort" and "generation," though often used interchangeably, are not exactly the same. A generation is usually defined by its years of birth. Cohorts are better defined by events that occur at various critical points in the group's lifetime).

To make this information useful for fund-raisers, following is a synopsis of a number of demographic and psychographic theories concerning cohorts. Currently we are dealing with seven generational groupings or cohorts, spanning from before 1901 to those born today. I've combined the oldest groupings together as the numbers are extremely small, thus I believe that there are five age groups that are relevant for us to deal with.

As the developed world moves into a new century, our prime fund-raising audiences will be Depression babies, World War babies, Boomers, Busters, and Boomlets.

Depression Babies

Currently aged 60 and older, people born prior to 1935 have "civic" personalities—believing it is the role of the citizen to fit into society and make it better. Civics are today's activist elderly.

Civics came of age during the Great Depression, and many of them fought in World War II. Their shared experiences gave them two key characteristics: frugality and patriotism. They are the 20th century's confident, rational problem-solvers, the ones who have always known how to get big things done.

Civics have boundless civic optimism and a sense of public entitlement. Former boy and girl scouts, they volunteer and give because it is part of their inner image. They respect authority, leadership, civic-mindedness, and discipline.

Their preferred message style: rational and constructive, with an undertone of optimism.

Their financial style: Shaped by memories of the 1929 stock market crash and the Great Depression, they have cautious spending habits. Always mindful of the lessons of their childhood, their money personalities are conservative. They tend to be cash payers and distrust the technology of the "cashless" society.

Their key life events include the Great Depression and World War II.

Their preferred fund-raising methodologies: The Depression babies remain most comfortable with the older fund-raising methods: direct mail and the door-to-door campaign. In their younger years, pioneering fund-raising organizations like the March of Dimes introduced direct-mail fund-raising and door-to-door campaigns. Depression babies are more likely to give through the mail or at the door than giving through a Direct Response Television (DRTV) program, the telephone, or the Internet. They are used to personalized, local, volunteer-driven campaigns and still react best to personalized direct-response appeals. They are less aware and less critical of personalization techniques.

For so many nonprofit organizations, their direct mail database is overrepresented by Depression babies.

World War II Babies

Born between 1935 to 1945, this smaller group of "young elders" was taught to be silent, believing in the will of the group rather than in individuality. War babies growing up during the "war to end all wars" learned to be "seen but not heard." Followers rather than leaders, they will respond to appeals to their other-directed pluralism, trust in expertise, emulation of the young, and unquenched thirst for adventure. What type of "personality do they have?

Consensus builders rather than leaders, Silents give freely to charity, are inclined to see both sides of every issue, and believe in fair process more than final results. They are organization-loyal and value-oriented.

Their preferred message style: sensitive and personal, with an appeal to technical detail.

Their financial style: Their parents drilled the lessons of the Great Depression into them, but Silents reached adulthood in golden economic days, benefiting from real estate appreciation, a booming stock market, portable pensions, government entitlements, and inflation. Now in early retirement, many are willing to spend on themselves if not on charity. Their financial style is "save a little, spend a little."

Their key life events include: World War II and the dropping of the bomb on Hiroshima and Nagasaki; the Cold War as symbolized by the Berlin Wall; and Senator Joseph R. McCarthy as well as Marilyn Monroe.

Their preferred fund-raising methodologies: Like Depression babies, World War II babies feel most comfortable with the traditional fund-raising methods: direct mail and door-to-door fund-raising. They became used to personalized, local volunteer-driven campaigns and still react best to personalized direct-response appeals. They too are less aware and less critical of personalization techniques.

The direct mail database of many nonprofit organizations, is overrepresented by World War II babies.

Baby Boomers

Our society's adult "idealists" (born between 1946 and 1964) have been hard for the world to swallow. Boomers were told they could do anything. Life is a voyage of self-discovery. They display a bent toward inner absorption, perfectionism, and individual self-esteem. Taught from birth that they were special, Boomers believe in changing the world, not changing to fit it. In midlife, they will see virtue in austerity and a well-ordered inner life. Also, they will demand a new assertion of community values over individual wants.

Their preferred message style: meditative and principled, with an undertone of pessimism. "They're the only generation that ended a war and fired a president," notes Barbara Caplan, vice president at Yankelovich Clancy Shulman, the marketing research firm. "To this day, they have a higher level of optimism, a sense that the world is their oyster." "This will be a much more open and challenging and possibly skeptical set of people," says marketer Rena Bartos on the aging of Baby Boomers.

Their financial style: Having always lived in a world of inflation and having no memories of the Great Depression, they have a different understanding of money. This is the generation that saw money lose clout. More is worth less. Financial planning is viewed as a sign of status in its own right. However, they are coming out of the free-spending 1980s to focus on nonmaterialistic values. They tend to buy first, pay later, and like monthly payment plans and using credit cards.

Their key life events include the assassinations of John and Robert Kennedy and Martin Luther King; worldwide rock music; the Red Brigade; and other campus/youth-based terrorism.

Their preferred fund-raising methodologies: Baby Boomers grew up with television and are more comfortable with that fund-raising medium than are Depression and World War II babies. In addition, they've come to accept the telephone as a method of giving. Finally, they are more aware of technological techniques in direct-response fund-raising and can be more cynical of their use than previous generations.

Baby Busters

The "reactive" young adults born between 1965 and 1977 are the first generation that doesn't believe life will be better for them than for their parents. Following the much-heralded boom, the media convinced us that Busters could do nothing right.

They were the throwaway children of divorce and poverty, the latchkey kids. Reactives weren't trusted or appreciated as youth and carry the scars into adulthood. They are the most Republican-leaning youths of the 20th century. Busters will need convincing proof that an organization is reliable and will simplify rather than complicate their lives.

Their preferred message style: blunt and kinetic, with an appeal to brash survivalism. "I want us to be the generation that leads, that votes, that earns, that spends, that doesn't continue to let our parents fight our wars for us," notes Nicholas W. Nyhan, graduating senior, in a commencement speech at the University of Massachusetts at Amherst, Massachusetts. They see their role in life pragmatically. They want to fix things rather than change them. They are highly influenced by technology and television.

Their financial style: The Twentysomething has a different view of the the good life. Only 21 percent say the most important measure of living the good life is financial success, and a scant 4 percent believe that the criterion is owning a home. The rest are more concerned with the acquisition of intangibles: a rich family or spiritual life, a rewarding job, the chance to help others, and the opportunity for leisure and travel or for intellectual and creative enrichment.

Still being supported in adulthood by parents, many have high discretionary income they will give to charities they support. Highly computer literate, they prefer the cashless society.

Their key life events include the crumbling of the Berlin Wall and opening of Eastern Europe; Ronald Reagan and Margaret Thatcher (and the distrust of big government); the Challenger explosion; MTV.

Their preferred fund-raising methodologies: This is a true television generation. They are more comfortable picking up the phone to give and are more comfortable with television as the medium to persuade them to give. In addition, they are the early adopters in giving on-line, but for them the Internet is something new, not something they've grown up with since they were young.

Baby Boomlet

The "civic" children of boomers, born from 1978 through 1996, hold many of the values of an earlier generation. While it may be too early to tell what events in their lives will be significant, it is likely that technology and globalism will play important roles. These kids are really into environment issues, recycling, and the like. They are growing up in a world without boundaries and are likely to extend their philanthropy well past their own national boundaries.

Their preferred fund-raising methodologies: The Internet is their future giving medium. Nonprofit organizations are already experiencing high school gifts—large numbers of teenagers are making small gifts and pledges on-line, especially on Web sites that have youth-focused fund-raising activities like World Vision's 48-hour famine event. They find direct mail very uncool!

How to Best Reach Divergent Audiences

As we move from our traditional civic and silent audiences, donor loyalty cannot be assumed to be the norm: Baby Boomers are the least "brand loyal" of the population cohorts.

This stems from their lifelong competition for resources and recognition. Having been told since childhood they were special, yet having faced the realities of overcrowding in every aspect of their personal and professional lives, Boomers tend to seek out reassurances that you see them as special. They expect to be treated as unique even when their level of involvement with a charity is modest. Boomers expect organizations seeking their patronage to cultivate them extensively.

Many organizations make an erroneous assumption that donor loyalty is the norm. Once the prospect makes a gift, the charity relaxes, believing it has acquired an annual donor. The major societal shifts going on make such an assumption dangerous.

Today people can have their own version of nearly any product. Many products and services are hyperpersonalized to seem made only for an individual. In fund-raising, computer technologies have made us overeager to embrace personalization with direct-response vehicles. In fact, the idea has contributed to a backlash from today's more sophisticated Boomer prospects. They are not fooled by the marvels of computerization into believing "this message's just for you."

Over the next 20 years, many experts believe that information technology may change more than it has over the last 200 years: Everyone wants to know more about everything. For example, on-line donors can view the computer code below the surface of your home page, explaining to them some of the programming you've built to take care of their personalized needs. Imagine, it's as if every direct-mail donor could look right inside your direct-mail plans. It's empowering for the donor but a little scary for the future development officer. Will it mean a new level of transparency in fund-raising techniques unheard of in the past and the present?

Nonprofits and charities have lagged far behind businesses in understanding how the changes in both population and technology have led donors and prospects to expect different solicitation techniques and methodologies.

Don Peppers and Martha Rogers, writing in *The One to One Future: Building Relationships One Customer at a Time,* caution that "The old paradigm, a system of mass production, mass media, and mass marketing, is being replaced by a totally new paradigm, a one-to-one economic system." In the past and right up to the present, economies of scale have always been important in fund-raising and reaching different audiences. Almost every nonprofit organization has needed to reach a certain number of supporters in a particular category before it could afford to contact them in a personalized way—taking into account personalized information.

The advent of new technologies in fund-raising, such as the Internet, means that economies of scale will never again be as important as they are today. John Groman, senior vice president of Epsilon (a database marketing company), agrees that the increasingly affordable economics of communication technology is driving this fund-raising/technological shift to: less direct mail because of its high cost, increasing flexibility of the printed medium, and availability of interactive media.

Mal Warwick, writing in *Technology and the Future of Fundraising,* predicts that "the business of direct mail fund-raising is changing in genuinely fundamental ways under the onslaught of new technologies—inter-networking, "multimedia," wireless communications, etc. Our appeals will need to be individualized, multi-sensory, information-rich, immediate, interactive, and communal." See Warwick's predictions in Chapter 1.

New information technologies have created an information-saturated environment where every citizen can know almost anything (through the Internet, TV, radio, and print) on any topic. One could say that organizations are practicing information age marketing whose mantra could be: "Tell, tell, tell, before you start to sell, sell, sell."

Baby Boomers have been called "information junkies" and "ominvores for information." They'll devour anything put in front of them, but they especially want specific information on the issues that interest them. However, they are too sophisticated to respond to intense, emotional appeals.

This means that low-key "telling" is going to increasingly replace high-pressure "selling" as the most effective way to get through to jaded consumers as we move further along in the transition from mass marketing to individualized marketing.

Nonprofit organizations also need to notice the major paradigm shift around financial technology: Midlife individuals and younger adults are letting go of checks and cash and using more credit cards and computers to pay bills, including gifts and charitable giving.

This is good news for nonprofits because it's been the traditional look at the checkbook balance that's kept gift amounts low. Few people are comfortable writing a single large check for charity. Not because they don't care, but rather because they think they can't afford the gesture.

Both Depression and World War II Babies tend to be cash payers, distrusting new technologies. These are the generations that still "tuck" emergency cash into wallets and handbags, and many of them prefer a "hands-on" arrangement with bill paying. In addition, many of them are uncomfortable using ATMs and other "modern" technologies. They are most likely to choose one-time check writing. Major gift giving to them means selling or giving away an asset—solid, real gifts, not something that only exists electronically.

Depression and World War II Babies tend to listen to society's recommendations and like to support traditional, well-established charities.

Mature donors will continue to prefer traditional methods of fund-raising and fulfillment. Those over 50 are the most literate individuals and actually enjoy receiving well-presented direct mail.

Boomers and younger people grew up in a different world. They tend to prefer the "cashless society," using credit cards, standing bank drafts, and electronic transfer. Younger donors are the heaviest users of debit cards: nearly one-quarter (24 percent) of people ages 18 to 23 have debit cards, as do 22 percent of those ages 35 to 54; only 12 percent of respondents age 55 or older have them, according to a Gallup Organization survey.

As they understand that their lifespan is likely to take them well into their 90s, few will make major gifts from assets. Major gift giving will take place by bequest instead. To pay for larger gifts they'll turn to time payments—just as they pay for everything else; that's their preferred fund-raising methodology.

Baby Busters are quite philanthropic but see themselves as having only small amounts of disposable cash to give to charity. (Their priorities include sharing with a large extended family of friends and concerts). Their gift fulfillment needs to be structured to allow for a constant stream of extremely modest gift amounts.

The paradigms are changing and we must change with them. As we move ahead into the new century, we will need to segment not only prospect audiences, but also fund-raising methodologies and your fulfillment options.

The marketing matrix for methodologies and fulfillment will look somewhat like this:

AUDIENCE	FUNDRAISING METHODOLOGY	FULFILLMENT OPTION
Mature Donors (50 +)	Face to face Direct mail	Checks or one-time gifts of assets made during life via planned giving and bequests
Mid-Age Donors (30–50)	Face to face Telephone TV/Video*	Pledges over time and one-time gifts via credit cards; major gifts via bequest only
Younger donors (18–30)	Computer networks	Continuous gifts via electronic fund transfer and bank draft; use of debit cards rather than credit cards; little hope of major gifts

The convergence of TV and the Internet through services like WebTV may make the Internet a more comfortable medium for Baby Boomers.

Personalizing for the Audience

To make a direct-response campaign work, every nonprofit organization needs to take into account the different demands of each audience. This isn't a trend, it's a must for future success in direct-response fund-raising. To help you understand this new strategic fund-raising necessity, I've included three approaches to consider:

1. Upgraded direct-response mail
2. Telecommunications appeals
3. Using the Internet

1. Upgraded Direct-Response Mail (Mature Donors)

Older individuals are still the most direct-mail responsive of our audiences. They have faith in our institutions and often see direct mail as "an invitation to adventure." Organizations know their older supporters will respond to a well-crafted letter in their mailbox, but there is more mail out there than ever before. How do you differentiate your message from the clutter in the mailbox?

The San Diego Zoo in California decided that "cheap is out," and uses expensive mailings that cost between $3.50 and $4 per piece to move first-time members to higher donor ties. According to Epsilon, the consulting company that formulated the zoo's approach, "packages like these mailed to the right audiences are very cost effective for a wide variety of groups." Epsilon has guided the zoo's direct mail campaign for more than 15 years.

Members receive mail from the zoo at least 16 times a year. Not all of the mailings are solicitations. *Zoonooz*, a monthly, four-color magazine with in-depth reports on the facility's residents, and *Zoo Log*, a quarterly newsletter detailing activities and special events, reinforce the partnership between members and the zoo. Similarly, a "membership appreciation brochure"—with coupons for free rides on the aerial tram and complimentary admission to the children's zoo—tell supporters they count.

The renewal notices and the publications encourage people to become involved in the Zoo's mission: insuring survival of some of the world's rarest animals.

The zoo sponsors several higher-level membership clubs with distinctive logos and identifications. These clubs stress exclusivity: members receive R.S.V.P. invitations to renew or join a higher-level club and "privileges" instead of "benefits." Mailings are oriented more toward a feeling of partnership with zoo staff members and less toward free passes and parking and various types of discounts. Club members get "insider" information, certificates of appreciation, and identification pins in the mail.

In addition to its regular membership and club appeals, the zoo does holiday and special-gift appeals. Each reinforces the "we" feeling. The thick holiday package, mailed in October, encourages members to purchase first-level memberships for friends and family. Attractive cards announcing the gift are enclosed. The special-gift appeals help the zoo's development staff identify contributors at the top of the donating ladder: those who can be targeted for legacy gifts.

The key to the success of the San Diego Zoo's direct mail is the organization's willingness to create a feeling of partnership—especially successful with the older supporters who still believe they can have a special relationship with an organization through a medium they've grown up trusting: the mail. Remember, they sent love letters, got important war messages, and heard about births and deaths through the mail. Their romance with the medium never went away, and the zoo has emphasized romance and adventure in its strategies.

2. Telecommunications Appeals (Midlife Donors)

Today's midlife individual (the Baby Boom generation born between 1946 and 1964) has a different information profile than its predecessors. Raised in the era of television, s/he is impatient with slower methods of receiving information and suspicious of direct mail. Videos (rarely used by nonprofits) are a good way of breaking through their media "clutter." Boomers prefer face-to-face and phone conversations.

Video Fund-raisers generally have neglected to use videotape, but this case study reminds us we should use it, especially with Boomers.

In 1996 a U.S. prison reform charity decided to appeal to its best donors. It segmented out its best donors (people who had given single or multiple gifts totaling $500 to $10,000 in the previous years).

It followed the following six strategies in the intense appeal:

1. Telemarketing research on what people thought about the project they were going to raise money for
2. Datafile analysis to choose the best donors for this multimedia appeal
3. First package to go out was an information update only

4. Second package was an appeal with one specific amount and gave them the *opportunity to order a video*
5. A telemarketing follow-up came two weeks after appeal and asked if donor got video, if ordered
6. A newsletter was sent two months later telling donor what was accomplished in appeal campaign

The organization chose 6,206 donors to mail. The response rate was 30.5 percent for a gross return of $1,305,324. The average gift was $690. The total appeal cost $184,000, so the net return was around $1,100,000. Your numbers would be proportionately smaller but no less profitable per donor.

The video lasted 12 minutes, with an emotive, personal but factual (good for Boomers!) appeal from the organization's founder. Nearly any nonprofit organization could create the same kind of appeal to its best donors.

Every nonprofit should attempt to address intensive communication with the right medium to the right audience.

Telephone Far too many fund-raisers neglect the telephone. Roger Craver, writing in *Fund Raising Management*, asserts that "use of the telephone is particularly helpful for upgrading donors on your house file, for welcoming and upgrading new donors to your organization, for alerting donors to special needs and emergencies, for thanking donors and for basic research into the needs and interests of individual donors." Baby Boomers are a key target audience; older individuals do not tend to make phone gifts. Society reinforces their reticence by running media stories about telephone fraud against seniors.

Fund-raisers and organization board members often hesitate to use the telephone, fearing it will be viewed as invasive. And although many people insist they hate telephone solicitations—up to 60 percent of consumers say they won't listen to an unsolicited sales pitch on the telephone—it works. As Ken Burnett, writing in *Relationship Fundraising*, reminds us so eloquently: How many people get out of the bathtub to answer a letter?

Charities have used thousands of combination direct-mail and telephone programs throughout the United States, Canada, and Europe. In this telecommunications method, success is measured by how many successful "closings" are accomplished. (In telemarketing, in contrast, success is measured by how many contacts can be made in a defined period of time.) In other words, combination programs are looking for quality contacts not the sheer volume of contact.

While the process works best when the prospective donor has a known relationship with the soliciting organization—an alumnus of a school, a former patient, a relative of a member of a religious order, a "family" member in some other identifiable way—acquisition programs based on lists with demographics similar to current members (age, postal code, income, educational level, even the magazines they read) have proven effective. The method is most effective when used for moving "family" members to first-time contributors, restarting lapsed donors, and upgrading current contributors.

Many of the concerns regarding telephone appeals can be eliminated by preceding the phone call with a preapproach letter, explaining who will be called, why the call is being made, and when it can be expected. Great care should be taken in both designing and processing the letters. Typically, they are individually addressed and word processed. Often they are signed by hand or with a signature machine, hand-stamped, and sent via first-class mail. Every component looks like a personal solicitation as far as possible degree: no indicia, no mass-printed letter, no metered mail, no third-class stamp. This is part of the cultivation process, designed to send the message "We treat you as an individual."

After the preapproach mailing, a trained caller places the phone call. The call is used for fulfillment and bonding. It is a dialogue centered around a series of questions that cannot easily be answered with a yes or a no. "How do you feel about the needs that were presented by Mr. X in his letter to you?" "How do you feel about the suggested level of giving Ms. X has proposed?" The prospect, approached in this way, has the opportunity to have a conversation with the caller—the essence of face-to-face solicitation. Because combination direct-mail and telephone programs follow the steps of the face-to-face solicitation process, potential donors receive two significant messages:

1. Their commitment is important to the organization both in terms of participation and size.
2. The organization views their commitment seriously and is willing to take time to finalize the pledge, even if that takes a series of cultivation/solicitation steps.

How well do combination direct-mail and telephone program work? Organizations report higher pledges and pledge rates than those using traditional letter–alone or phone call–alone direct-response programs. Although the focus of these programs are the lower-end donor, participating organizations have reported major gifts ranging from million-dollar bequests to outright gifts of $10,000 and greater. Fulfillment rates are generally high, sometimes over 90 percent. For most organizations, the cost of the combination program is under 30 cents per dollar pledged, making it a very cost-effective vehicle.

But what happens when you combine the telephone, or live human contact, with the Internet? For the retail company Lands End, its Web site, www.landsend.com, offers prospective donors with the opportunity to use live chat with a service person if they have questions or reservations about buying their products. If Boomers are uncomfortable with making a purchase on-line, then they could talk to a live person via the telephone while on-line—or they could have a live chat with someone on-line.

Nonprofit organizations are also trying to combine a trusted medium, such as the telephone (or a live person via chat), with the Internet. Greenpeace International in Amsterdam is putting a live person on-line with its giving page. When people want to ask a question about making a donation on-line, they can pick up the phone and talk to the person pictured on the Web page (the membership director) or talk to them live, via Internet chat. Greenpeace hopes to allay the fears of Boomers so that they'll make a gift there on-line.

Greenpeace USA has a fine example of blending different mediums. When someone goes to make an on-line gift and clicks on "Ask Greenpeace Supporter Services," up pops a box that allows a prospective donor (a reticient Boomer?) to respond to a question and leave a time when he or she can be contacted via phone. The call center operating hours are also listed.

3. Using the Internet (Young Adults)

Because younger audiences prefer newer methods, organizations should plan on an increased use of electronic newsletters, videos, e-mail, and computer bulletin boards. Baby Busters and the Baby Boomlet are the first audiences that grew up with computerization, and they expect to use the computer for their own philanthropy. Computer programs now allow people to look at information, interact by (for example) taking a brief quiz, and send for information on charities interest them.

The Chronicle of Philanthropy reported on the Internet NonProfit Center, run entirely by volunteers. The center was set up by Buster Cliff Landesman, a graduate student at Princeton University, to make it "faster, cheaper, and easier" for donors to learn about charities. Using the center, you can peruse the "Best Buys for Big Hearts" list of the top charities in various categories, such as the environment or youth, as ranked by the American Institute of Philanthropy, a watchdog organization based in St. Louis. The institute bases its ranking on the percentage of a group's income that goes to charitable programs. You can also retrieve a "donor's defense kit" that includes tips on "how to say 'no' without guilt," electronic versions of charity annual reports, and suggestions about how to obtain more information on charities.

Other "roadmaps" are springing up to help potential donors navigate the Internet:

• Ellen Spertus, a Massachusetts Institute of Technology graduate student now at Microsoft Corporation, first helped the Global Fund for Women. She then set up a list of nonprofit information sites that runs on software that uses the World Wide Web technology. With a few clicks of a computer mouse, reports *The Chronicle*, people can automatically be connected to the Internet site that has the information they want.

• ReliefNet is a new network that provides information on international relief efforts, offers users a way to make a pledge electronically to the group(s) of their choice, and serves as a link to other information about relief efforts posted on the Internet. Jack Hidary, director of Earth Web and creator of the ReliefNet, notes that most donors to relief groups tend to be over 40. "ReliefNet is a means of conveying to another generation the work that's being done."

The key to the future of direct-response fund-raising is to take advantage of new technologies in new mediums. These new mediums will eliminate the past restrictions to one-to-one communication because of economies of scale and allow us to deliver information and build friend-raising/fund-raising relationships with younger audiences that demand more intimate and empowering relationships with nonprofit organizations.

Using the Database to Understand, Secure, and Keep Future Donors

Jeff Gignac

Is There a Trend with Databases in Direct-Response Fund-Raising?

In so many areas of fund-raising, technological changes have been adopted and used to improve techniques and endeavors. Technological changes in the area of communications have given nonprofits the ability to have a closer, more involved relationship with each donor.

Technology is inspiring nonprofit organizations to offer donors their choice of communication—through the Internet, the telephone, the mail, or person to person. We can get back to donors faster and more accurately (if they have concerns, questions, or comments) than ever before, and we know more about them through computerized (and now instanteous) surveys.

Today there are fewer and fewer excuses for fund-raising that is generic, cold, or mass marketing at its worst.

And the building blocks for improved, personalized fund-raising in this new millennium lies with the computerized database. Databases are becoming more powerful and capable of creating stronger relationships between a nonprofit donor by uncovering the connections between actions, needs, and desires.

Nonprofit managers need to understand what these databases are capable of doing before they can use them to improve and (in some cases) revolutionize their direct-response fund-raising.

More Than Just a Card Filing System

Many nonprofit organizations currently use computerized databases much like they used their card files, which were replaced by the computer—to store the name and address of the donor (and maybe gift amounts). Most organizations simply use their current computer database to sort their lists by name and perhaps by size of gift or recency of gift.

However, many fund-raisers have become aware that we all need to go beyond using our database systems only to capture names, addresses and giving history. But not everyone knows that we should be looking toward the strategic development of the information we capture and how to implement this new and powerful source into our fund-raising activities. Good strategic development includes what makes a good database, donor development, prospect research, segmentation of data, solicitation tracking, monthly donor programs, electronic funds transfer, bar code scanning, telemarketing, and the Internet.

It's about doing our homework as quickly, efficiently, and cost effectively. Most of all, though, it's about getting back to people and finding out more about them to match their interests with our work. The database is the key to realizing the potential of building relationships with supporters.

It's important to remember that direct-response fund-raising is not to be isolated from other areas of fund-raising. For a long time, special-event donors were kept away from direct-mail donors who were separated from major gift or planned givers. The increasing power and sophistication of relational databases has to be a wake-up call to all fund-raisers.

Technological tools now allow us to understand how a donor relates to an organization (often with a sophisticated and complex set of entry points, such as a volunteer, event goer, newsletter subscriber, and monthly donor), and we need to adopt values, initiatives, and fund-raising practices that recognize this fact. If nonprofit organizations fully understand the basics, best practices, and advanced abilities of computer databases, then they'll be ready to fully understand what a donor wants from a nonprofit organization: a close, understanding, stimulating relationship.

If nonprofit organizations are in a more competitive fund-raising environment, then their donors will be receiving fund-raising appeals from other nonprofit organizations that understand how their database can treat donors in a personal, appealing way. Every nonprofit needs to understand how its database can help it understand, secure, and keep future donors.

Before we can look at trends and case studies, we need to make sure everyone starts from the same place.

Mastering the Basics: Not Letting the Technology Submerge What's Most Important

What Is a Database?

This isn't a simple question to answer anymore. It isn't just the electronic files sitting on one of your computers. That's the software and hardware side of things. The healthy trend today is to move beyond the definition that a database is a collection of donor records. It should also be about the people who believe in your work enough to support you. A database should be central not only to your organizational objectives but also to all of your fund-raising activities. Information technology is not just what is on your computer but the processes that surround it, from paper files to the Internet.

Once there was the typewriters; then came word processing, which many people used as a simple extension of the typewriter; then databases became more commonly used, and still many people worked with them as an extension of their word processor. Now there is the Internet. The time has come to create a flow of information that can be accessed easily within your database that is well beyond the capabilities of the word processor or typewriter.

Many charities wonder whether they need a database. The simple answer is yes. No organization is ever too small to enjoy the benefits of a database. In fact, it's the small organizations that sometimes will reap the most benefits of a database.

Does Size Matter; Are Greater Numbers Better? The benefits of the database are more apparent to medium-size to large organizations. Often smaller organizations track only names and address for tax-receipting purposes. That is a great start. But a database can do more than just issue tax receipts.

The size of your database is not what is important. There are advantages and disadvantages to both large and small numbers. A small database lists a small core group of donors who are interested in a cause; the organization can provide personal attention to those donors. Fewer donors enable an organization to focus on building effective relationships with them, which can have a greater return than some larger systems.

The greater the number of records, the more chance there is to have problems such as lapsed donors and out-of-date information. Sheer numbers make it more difficult to focus on individuals and provide personal attention. The key is to segment these donors into a format that enables the organization to focus on the best prospects.

Features of a Good Database

A good database should have clean, accurate, and consistent data. The procedure for processing donations should be reviewed regularly. Is information entered consistently? Does everyone follow the same standards, use the same institutional shorthand, and know whom to turn to for help in making decisions about information that he or she is not sure how to capture?

In-house Database Guidelines   If the data entered are not consistent and they have not been reviewed, problems could arise; relationships with donors could be threatened. Everyone who uses databases should be familiar with the rules and guidelines for data entry. It's one thing to have donation processing staff use these guidelines; however, *everyone* who enters information into the database should be familiar with them.

In-house database guidelines contain a common language and best practices that will meet the organization's needs. What goes into the database will have a direct impact on what comes out and how it comes out. Getting together all of the key stakeholders to discuss and develop the guidelines for data entry builds their understanding and commitment to the process and, ultimately, the database. This understanding includes the importance of why rules must be followed and the consequences if they are not adhered to.

Salutations and Addressing Donors   Consistent data do not just mean address information. Donors must be addressed consistently in letters and receipt. This consistency is crucial to how your donor will perceive your respect and acknowledgment of their support. This is best accomplished by treating each donor record separately, which means using a unique salutation and not a global standard for each donor.

Have a way of addressing the donor at the top of a letter. This could be just the donor, as in Mr. John M. Smith. It could also be as the couple, Mr. and Mrs. John M. Smith. The organization should also be able to handle other situations, as when a couple is not married, for example, Mr. John M. Smith and Ms. Mary K. Jones.

Proper salutation after the "dear" is just as important. Depending on the donor, a more formal salutation, such as Mr. Smith or Mr. and Mrs. Smith, could be used. Based on who is signing the letter, it may be more appropriate to use a first name or even a nickname, for example, John or Skip. The salutation after the "dear" should always match the format used in the address. For example, if you had Mr. John Smith and Mrs. Mary Smith as the addressee, you should then have Mr. Smith and Mrs. Smith as the salutation. A salutation of Mr. and Mrs. Smith would be considered bad form.

Always be prepared to handle special requests. Many donors would be addressed as Mr. and Mrs. Smith. But perhaps they prefer to have their tax receipts signed Mrs. Susan Smith. If many donors prefer this salutation, proper coding in the system is important.

Exhibit 4.1 is a sample addressee and salutation chart. This chart could be used as a starting point for discussions with the donation processing staff and the rest of the development office.

EXHIBIT 4.1 Addressee and Salutations Standards

Situation	Solution
Married Couple —Man signed the check	Addressee: Mr. & Mrs. Robert Smith Salutation: Mr. & Mrs. Robert Smith Tax Receipt: Mr. Robert Smith
Married Couple —Woman signed the check	Addressee: Mr. Robert Smith and Mrs. Mary Smith Salutation: Mr. and Mrs. Smith Tax Receipt: Mrs. Mary Smith
Common-law Couple —Man signed the check	Addressee: Mr. Robert Smith and Ms. Mary Jones Salutation: Mr. Smith and Ms. Jones Tax Receipt: Mr. Smith
Common-law Couple —Woman signed the check	Addressee: Mr. Robert Smith and Ms. Mary Jones Salutation: Mr. Smith and Ms. Jones Tax Receipt: Ms. Jones
Single or Individual	Addressee: Mr. Robert Smith Salutation: Mr. Smith Tax Receipt: Mr. Robert Smith
Organization Affiliation	Addressee: Mr. Robert Smith Salutation: Robert Tax Receipt: Mr. Robert Smith
Donor Gender Unknown	Addressee: Leslie Brown Salutation: Leslie Brown Tax Receipt: Leslie Brown
Family Relationships	Addressee: Ms. Mary Smith and Ms. Karen Jones Salutation: Ms. Smith and Ms. Jones Tax Receipt: Ms. Mary Smith
Family Relationships	Addressee: Mr. Robert Smith and Mr. George Smith Salutation: Mr. and Mr. Smith Tax Receipt: Mr. George Smith
Business or Organization with a Contact	Addressee: Mr. James Anderson Salutation: Mr. Anderson Tax Receipt: ABC Company Ltd.

Case Study: The Ontario March of Dimes   The Ontario March of Dimes created a more detailed structure for handling donations. They used the chart presented in Exhibit 4.1 and created more specific examples based on the mail they received. Working closely with the donation processors themselves, they reviewed the different pieces of mail that were received in one day for combinations of names and signatures. Anytime they discovered a new combination that did not exist previously, it was added to their selection.

Important Trends and Abilities to Layer on Top of the Basics

Database Segmentation

Database segmentation is becoming more commonly known as part of data mining. Database segmentation is the process of selecting and exploring donation records to uncover donors' giving patterns. The following four questions should be asked to begin the segmentation process.

1. Who are the top n donors? (where n is 20, 50, 100)
2. How many active donors do we have? (Active donors are donors who have given in the last two years or some other time frame as you decide.)
3. How many lapsed donors do we have? (Lapsed donors are donors who have not given between two to three years or some other time frame as you decide.)
4. How many dormant donors do we have? (Dormant donors are donors who have not given in the last four years or more, or some other time frame as you decide.)

When segmenting the database, four types of donors should be excluded.

1. Donors who are deceased or for whom no current address is available
2. Donors who are members of a donor-giving club.
3. Donors who have a closer relationship to your organization. (e.g., board members, etc.)
4. Certain types of prospects who deserve more closer handling. (e.g., major or planned gift prospects.)

Identifying these two groups of records is the first step in segmenting data for a mailing. Then begin to segment data into more targeted areas relative to the organization's work and objectives. Once all the targeted segments are described, solicitation tracking should be implemented.

Solicitation Tracking

Many executive directors and board members ask: How well is our direct mail doing? Another frequently asked question is: How was the cost per dollar raised on the prospect mailing? Both these questions can be answered by reviewing solicitations.

Solicitation tracking is the heart of many fund-raising programs. Every interaction you have with a donor or prospect can be called a solicitation. Whether it's a newsletter, an annual report, or a specific mailing, they are all vehicles for receiving donations.

A solicitation can be broken down not only by type, house, or prospect but also by segment. Each segment should be tracked separately. By doing so, the following seven questions can be answered:

1. What was the total revenue for this segment?
2. Were we over or under our goal for this segment?
3. What is our response rate?
4. What was our total cost?
5. What is our cost per dollar raised?
6. What is our cost per piece?
7. What is our cost per solicitation?

When preparing for a solicitation, whether it is a newsletter, a direct mail piece, or a special event, make sure to keep track of all costs. After the mailing has been completed, you will have the statistics from your database to determine the costs of the whole mailing as well as for each segment.

For example, say you are doing a house mailing to 20,000 donors to four segments (a, b, c, and d) and the total cost of the mailing (including printing, postage, etc.) is $16,000. The following chart illustrates each segment, the number of records in each segment, and the cost per segment.

List	Number of Donors	Multiplier	Cost
House 1A	4,000	0.20	$ 3,200
House 1B	8,500	0.425	$ 6,800
House 1C	3,000	0.15	$ 2,400
House 1D	4,500	0.225	$ 3,600
Total	20,000	1	$16,000

To determine the multiplier, take the number of donors in the segment and divide by the total. In the example, House 1A, we divide the total number of donors (4,000) we are mailing into 20,000. This will give us a multiplier of 0.20. We take the multiplier and multiply by the total cost of the mailing, $20,000. This result, $3,200, is the total cost of this segment.

Once the mailing goes out and the donations are being processed, the data entry needs to include each corresponding solicitation. This will allow a determination of how well each segment in the appeal performed.

Monthly Donor Programs

One of the ultimate goals of any fund-raising program is to move the donor or prospect to become a monthly donor. There are two different ways donors can give monthly; either directly on their credit card or directly from their bank accounts.

Electronic Funds Transfer (EFT)   One of the new areas into which charities are moving is processing donations made through electronic funds transfer (EFT). EFT donations are recurring donations made on a donor-specified time frame, such as monthly or quarterly, from their bank account. With an EFT donation, donors commit to a certain amount to be withdrawn from their bank account at the same time each period.

Once donors agree to the electronic transaction, they need to send in void checks. Each void check will contain all the information you need to send to the bank. The bank will in turn communicate with donors' banks to withdraw the money from their accounts to be placed directly into the organization's account.

When setting up the EFT transaction in a database, certain pieces of information must be captured such as the donor's bank name and branch plus account number. The bank name and branch information is captured in the transit number. This number tells your bank which bank the donor has the account with and where the account resides.

Once the bank account information is set up for the donor, the recurring transaction must be recorded. The recurring transaction will define when the donation should be withdrawn from the donor's account. When setting up the EFT transactions, ensure the correct fund (or designation of the donation) is tracked correctly. Also track the date the recurring transaction was agreed to with the donor and the payment schedule.

The recurring schedule will define when the donation will be withdrawn from the donor's bank account. Some donors may have a time frame established to give a monthly donation, so track that information carefully. Donors will be upset if an organization tries to take money out of their account after they have told you to stop making the recurring donation. The final piece will be the frequency of the donation. Some donors may want to make more than one recurring donation. The system should allow for multiple recurring donations.

Once the entire recurring EFT donation is ready to be transmitted to the bank, you just need to coordinate with your bank. Some banks have a standard format for transmitting; in Canada, several banks (but not all) support the 1464 file format. In the United States, most banks follow a common format for transmission.

Test the transmission with the bank to ensure it can receive the EFT-generated file. This file will contain all the information the bank will need to withdraw money from donors' accounts. If you do not test the transmission, then you run the risk of the file not being correct and delaying the actual withdrawal and ultimately the transfer of funds to your account.

Not every transaction sent to the bank will result in money for the organization. For whatever reason, withdrawal from some donors' accounts may be denied. Deal with those exceptions prior to entering the donation on the donor's record. Do not post a donation that was not made to a record, which otherwise the organization could incorrectly issue a tax receipt for that donation.

Credit Card Donations The other way donors can make recurring donations is via their credit card. A lot of the basic principles of EFT donations apply to credit card donations. The system will need way to record the credit card information along with the authorization code. With credit card transactions, there will be separate authorization codes for each period the donation is placed. You must also take into account when someone no longer wants the donation to be placed on to his or her credit card.

Save the Children—Canada

Save the Children—Canada has approximately 1,200 monthly electronic fund transfer donors and about 500 monthly credit card donors. These donors have elected to sponsor children in various countries. The electronic fund transfer module is a very convenient way for the donors to maintain their sponsorship and their ongoing support that specifically matches their interests.

Save the Children—Canada tracks all monthly donors in its fund-raising management system. The organization can look at donor records and see individual histories of giving. It also can track future projected income since it has these committed donors on the system and can project the revenues based on the expected donations.

Daily Credit Card Donations

Most organizations receive credit card donations as part of their normal daily mail. Third-party packages allow an organization to interface with credit card companies and validate the credit cards on-line or through a batch process. By validating the credit cards at the time they are being processed, cards that are declined can be dealt with immediately, without having to wait until later.

The Baycrest Centre Foundation

The Baycrest Centre Foundation in Toronto, Canada, has two main areas that require credit card donation processing. One is the donation office, where they receive phone calls from people making donations in honor or in memory of someone. The other is the cashier who handles all the checks and some credit card payments. Both of these departments create batches in their fund-raising management system. At the end of the day, the batches are validated for accuracy. Cybercash (www.icverify.com) then processes the credit card donations through a third-party software service program, IC Verify. This program validates the card and receives the authorization from the credit card company. If the card is declined, the declining reason is recorded instead of the authorization number.

Someone from the foundation then telephones the donor to inform him or her that the card was declined and the donation was not authorized. The donor can then give a new credit card number or elect to pay the outstanding amount via check.

Prospect Research

Research is the cornerstone of the fund-raising operation. It is estimated that research represents over 80 percent of the work involved in securing a gift. This applies to individuals, companies, and foundations. Research supports all fund-raising activities and leads to more successful solicitations. The fundamental success of research depends on a well-developed relational fund-raising database system.

Research is the basis for identifying prospects and the appropriate types of approaches to reach them. As new donors are secured, new avenues to prospects are opened up. An effectively planned research program consists of a number of different tools besides the database. These include desk, market, and Internet research, strategic targeting; and the preparation of background documents such as profiles, briefings, and approach strategies.

Exhaustive research leads into networking, which is the key to ensure that the right approaches are being made in the best way possible. This kind of research includes the ongoing input, maintenance, and update of the information held on a relational database, which is critical for targeting and analysis of prospective and current donors.

Consistent use of reporting systems and infrastructure to ensure two-way communication of information between all levels of a organization locally, regionally, and nationally from staff to volunteers and board members is crucial. Collate the information captured as quickly as possible and ensure that legal guidelines and regulations are followed. Remember to be accountable for research and the details entered on the database, especially as these can include such personal information as people's interests, who knows whom, how well, and how they actually know them.

Research Strategy A prospect research strategy should include the following:

- A fund-raising-biased press cutting service
- Access to the Internet
- A library of relevant directories, books, and publications
- A fund-raising relational database system

Any effective research strategy needs a regularly updated database system to be used to coordinate, facilitate, and search for relationship links to potential prospects and known donors. This includes producing research lists of prospects and donors, which will serve as the basic tool for securing information to identify top prospects. The prospect list could include any of the following:

- Past and current donors
- Contacts of past and current supporters
- Donors to other similar campaigns and charities
- Major corporate and community donors

- Prospects with stated interests that match the organization's work
- Companies, organizations, and individuals previously approached with nil return
- Wealthy individuals and high-profile individuals

Research Objectives
- Acquire available resources with a fund-raising perspective, such as press cuttings, library of directories, Internet, files, and fund-raising database system.
- A good relational *database* for research and analysis makes all this more efficient and more effective, and easier.
- *Analyze* the database for information to build strategies and directions to meet short-term and long-term fund-raising objectives.
- *Identify* prospects starting with your own donors. Research their background and history and find ways to approach them.
- *Manage* and regularly update information to coordinate, facilitate and search for links through relationships for prospects and donors as well as to avoid blind duplicate approaches.
- Grow relationships and support of your own donors through *donor development*.
- Through research find *new prospects* who might be interested in the organization work.
- *Match* prospect interests with the organization's own.
- Use *personal intelligence gathering* and experience to confirm research and find out new details and names.
- Use *approach strategies* to define preliminary and to revise angles for asking. Always look for the best ask.

Fund-Raiser, Database, and Research

The ideal would be to capture and track all the information available on donors and prospects to get beyond address and giving details. Research is fundamental to enabling fund-raisers to have a complete picture of who they are, what they like, and what they will support. The aim is to track relationships between the organization and donors as well as their general interests, whom they might know, and their connections to companies and foundations.

Researching, growing and developing prospect information is an ongoing process. It can be challenging to capture it on one central database and to keep it up to date. An investment of time and resources is required in order to find out who donors and prospects really are. Everyone in fund-raising must be committed to the importance of research. You need to know about your donors and match their interests with your work.

Best-Practice Rules in Research

Research and fund-raising are more than information and doing one's homework, they are about people. Remember these seven rules:

1. You will come across some very personal information.
2. Be wary as some of it will be gossip; do not add to it or spread it further.
3. Make sure that you are accountable, ethical, and moral about what you learn and know about your donors and prospects.
4. Respect the privilege of what information brings.
5. Abide by relevant laws and regulations regarding privacy and information.
6. Be aware that in most countries, people have a right to see all that you have recorded about them.
7. Set up your own "best practices"—do not record in any format, whether on paper or computers, any information that might be considered libelous or detrimental to these laws and regulations.

Organizations such as the National Society of Fund Raising Executives (www.nsfre.org), the Institute of Charity Fundraising Managers, and the Association of Professional Researchers for Advancement (www.apra.org) all play an active role in the area of ethics.

In addition, regulation of the Internet will play a large part in the future, not only at home, but worldwide. Some laws already are some in place. For example, in the United Kingdom and Europe there are strong regulations under the Data Protection Act. Some people might view this as putting too many restrictions and limits on what can be captured regarding to research information. However, protecting the rights of others is vital. Janice Marini, research and operations manager of the Royal National Institute for the Blind, recounted in a December 1999 telephone interview.

At the Royal National Institute for the Blind (RNIB) in the United Kingdom, we are committed to building relationships with current donors and finding new prospects to fund our projects. Research plays an essential role in this process, affording us a more complete picture of donor interests, patterns of giving, and company or foundation links.

Ideally, we would like an integrated database that captures and tracks all prospect information beyond mere address details. We at RNIB are working to achieve this, while simultaneously ensuring that these records comply with the Data Protection Act in Europe. It's challenging work, but absolutely essential if we are to succeed in our fund-raising.

Donor Development

Today's charities are wont to track more information about their donors— their interests, likes, dislikes, hobbies, friends, colleagues, whom do they know. All this information should be tracked in the database and developed on an ongoing basis.

Donor development is about building a two-way, evolving relationship with each of an organization's key donors and guide them to the next level of giving by looking at ways to increase their support, over longer periods of time, through to the ultimate gift—a planned gift.

It is about people and getting to know them better while giving them an opportunity to know an organization better in return. It bridges all of our activities and contacts with people from the direct-response program through to our services within every community. By looking at the bigger picture and the wider horizon, fund-raisers can be extremely successful.

Every attempt should be made to secure the continuing involvement of those who have given so that their interest and commitment is maintained. "Friends in high places" are a vital element in all fund-raising. Another way to keep donors and prospects involved is to link them to one another by using your database to find their mutual interests. This can be an extremely complex yet rewarding task.

Donor Development Is More than Donor Tracking   Donor development is based on building relationships with all key donors and taking them to the next level of giving, for example, five to ten times their current gift level. Some of these donors will have the propensity and capability to give even larger donations.

The research and details required to make notional value assessments on prospects and donors is an extremely complex task; often it is easier to look at the mixture of new prospects and donor development. Donor development consists of:

- Annual gifts and activities
- Planned giving and bequests
- Ongoing stewardship
- Relationship building—strategic program to develop their commitment
- Major gifts—next level of giving potentially leading up to the ultimate major gift: a planned gift

Research can identify who can give more and help you to plan the best method of approach. Follow these steps:

- Utilize not only the information research gives you but the guidance, experience, and internal knowledge of the researchers themselves.
- Listen to what key board members, volunteers, colleagues, and other donors have to say about the prospect as well as the information available from other sources.
- Coordinate planning between the fund-raisers and the researchers to develop an individualized approach strategy for each prospect.
- Base decisions on research to determine what to ask for.
- Capitalize on collective experience, information, and skills that fund-raisers researchers have to determine the best method of approach.

The success of donor development only comes through a holistic research approach as outlined above. This approach can lay a strong foundation for a longer-term major gifts or capital campaign.

What Is Donor Development?
- Elementary donor development is based on your existing donors—your best prospects are those who have already supported you.
- Usually on a direct marketing database.
- Encourage them to give you larger gifts.
- Increase their level of giving—encourage them to increase their current gift level.
- Upgrade donors by asking them to give more by mail.
- Secure longer-term commitments on a regular basis.
- Make sure donor development is an integral part of *all* your fund-raising activities—annual, direct mail, corporate, foundation, planned giving or major gifts

- Involve donors through public relations, public awareness, and "friend-raising" activities.
- Donor development is more than management, the art of crafting the approach, and the ask—it's relationship building, awareness building, and bringing donors closer to you.
- A combination of multiple, strategic, and personalized "touches" from strategically tailored and personalized written correspondence supplemented by telephone to meeting them in person.
- It's about changing from written to personal contact—the best way to solidify donors' commitment to you is in person, preferably with someone they know and respect for a cause they all believe in.
- Select key donors who have the propensity and ability to give.
- Implement a stewardship and recognition program.
- Relationship-building strategy to build their ongoing commitment to you.
- Strategically seek major gifts—10 percent of donors are major gifts prospects.
- Coordination is key, keep your eyes on the bigger picture and look for the "orbit" surrounding donors and their network of contacts.
- Find out those who could be door openers for you.
- Match new prospect names against your donor base to look for current supporters.
- Look into companies for multiple levels of support—donations as well as sponsorship and marketing potential partnerships.

The Red Cross:
A Study in Thoughtful Donor Research Development

As John Gray director of public affairs of the British Red Cross said in January 2000 telephone interview:

At the British Red Cross, we recognize that research is fundamental to enabling us to have a better understanding of the type of people who would be interested in our work. Taking the time to learn more about who they are and what they like is the foundation to being able to establish effective relationships together. The question is how do we effectively add to what we already learn from our Direct Mail and Special Events programmes.

Yes, it is an ongoing process to grow our donor development relationships. However, it can be challenging to balance the need for information with actually getting out and reaching our donors. Finding ways of using the

Internet to fundraise, let alone searching its vast depths for information, adds to the challenge.

At the British Red Cross, like many of our peers, we are committed to rising to the challenges ahead. We know what we need to do. We just have to do it.

Personal Contacts Increase the probability of fund-raising success by sharing researched names with people. A list is better than a blanket question "Tell me who you know"; show them who you are trying to reach, tell them why, and share your vision with them. A researched list of prospects from the database is a key tool to support this process.

Use these lists to open up dialogues and to find out what others know about prospects and whom you have missed. This can be an essential element for your donor development and to encourage donors to give more. It involves a strategic program to build relationships with these donors to maintain their interest and/or raise their level of giving.

Add additional names of new prospects from outside the database. Match new prospects against the database. Find those hidden gold prospects through high-quality research techniques.

Any name on a list or list of supporters should:

- Be treated as very private and confidential.
- Never be left behind or widely circulated with anyone outside of your staff team.
- Always be shared in person, never be mailed, faxed, or e-mailed.
- Consist of the current top donors—those who have given at a set level as a one-time gift or cumulatively.
- Be kept manageable and within the resources you have to service the donor development process.
- Be used to find out who can make approaches with you and/or for you.
- Include your staff and volunteers in reviewing these names.
- Help you to look for donors who are well networked and respected by their peers.
- Enable you to find out who knows whom, who is closest, and follow the best-ask principle—who is closest to the prospect, committed to you, and fits the right profile is the one who asks for the donation.

Always beware of gossip and treat it with due diligence and care!

Approach Strategies For each prospect, fund-raisers should have a specifically tailored approach strategy to match the person's interests and objectives with the organization's work. The process is to:

- Identify a selected target or group (wealthy individual, a foundation, a company) to whom you have an identified fund-raising route.
- Establish the most effective method of approach as determined by research, which will show your best opportunity for success.
- Prepare various reports and profiles including background information, relationship web—whom the prospect might know, giving history, interests in general, and other charitable giving as well as known financial circumstances.
- Provide a tailored case for that individual, company, or foundation to give support.
- Develop approach strategies and implement a series of contacts to begin to build ongoing relationships.
- Build on interest kindled and formalize the request for support.
- Activate an energetic follow-up for prospects before and after solicitation and build ongoing relationships.

A Seasoned Perspective on Treating a Donor as More Than a Number

As Pamela Brown Gignac, a fund-raising and research consultant for over 15 years in both the United Kingdom and Canada, said in a January 2000 conversation:

My work with clients both large and small both in the United Kingdom and Canada includes finding ways of tracking information on prospects that enables us to know more about them. The aim is to strategically approach people as well as companies and foundations—to stop and think about it first on a case-by-case basis. We do not want to "waste anyone's time" by activating inappropriate approaches to those whose interests do not match what we have to share. It really is about respecting them even before we meet them.

Research is key to showing us the way. The Internet has become a huge wealth of information. However, as use of the Internet grows, so does the scope of various ethical, moral, and legal issues that surround it. It's likely that other countries are either looking into this seriously or already have implemented similar regulations to the Data Protection Act. We have a responsibility in the not-for-profit sector to ensure that we are taking part in this area and addressing these issues.

All this takes time and money, which is difficult when both are often in short supply. Yet many realize that this investment is an important one to make. That's the first step; the next one is much harder—actually participating in it!

Bar Code Scanning

One of the new ways to enter donations into fund-raising management systems is bar code scanning. Bar codes are machine-readable symbols made of patterns of black and white bars and stripes that are placed on the reply card or donation form.

A fund-raiser could create an appeal with donor information encoded right on the appeal. This information could include donor name, donor-unique ID number, appeal or mailing segmentation ID, designation of the donation, and the like. When the donation is returned, it can be scanned directly into the fund-raising management system, thus reducing data entry time, eliminating duplication, and having more accurate donations.

Another area where bar codes could be used is in a museum or art gallery. Membership cards bearing bar codes could be scanned every time a member visits. This information could be recorded in the fund-raising management system and be used for reporting, solicitation, or tracking purposes.

A Centralized Database—All for One and One for All?

National charities are finding they cannot go it alone and are beginning to combine and coordinate their activities through one central database to be used by every member across the country. Up until now, national organizations consisted of regions, divisions, chapters, and locals, any number of which might have its own database and system for capturing information.

Even in small organizations, having one database and central process for capturing information makes sense in order to avoid blind duplicate approaches. It is not politic for more than one person to call the same individual or company asking for the same information about donation policies. Duplicate call recipients might be wondering whether members of your organization talk to each other.

Years ago, organizations kept information in different silos and assigned any number of people the same prospects. Each person would treat the prospect as his or her own personal property and territory instead of coordinating and sharing with colleagues. Such behavior becoming far less unacceptable to prospects, who comprise a limited resource pool and are becoming more sophisticated in their expectations of contacts with not-for-profits and fund-raisers.

As a result, more organizations are realizing they need to share information and coordinate their efforts. Fund-raising management system can do this by tracking the calls, approaches, contacts, giving policies, requests, and the asks to enable you to make a carefully planned strategic approach.

The best way to handle this in national charities is for the organization to have only one database for the entire organization. With the Internet and other costs decreasing everyday, it's not expensive for a development office at one end of the country to access the same database as another development office at the other end of the country. With one central database you can access and share the same information while keeping it up to date and coordinating approaches. Donors will be happier and so will prospects.

The Canadian Breast Cancer Foundation

The Canadian Breast Cancer Foundation (CBCF) created one fund-raising management system to be used across the country. Fund-raisers in Vancouver, Toronto, or Halifax would have the same access to the data.

The CBCF created a national wide area network and used the Citrix Winframe software to allow access to the data. The user in Vancouver would log on to the Citrix Winframe software and would then be able to access the database, just as the user in Halifax could.

Telemarketing

A lot of hospitals and other charities are involved in telemarketing programs. They take a potential list of donors or prospects and call to solicit them for a donation. Some use telemarketing software programs to track the prospects, their address, work details (if available), spousal information, and phone numbers. This information would then be used to call the donor and request the donation. The result of the phone call, either positive or negative, is tracked. If the call is positive—that is, if a donation is made—the information pertaining to the donation is also tracked.

This information is transferred either manually or electronically back into the existing fund-raising management system. The information is needed for tax receipts to be produced as well as for reporting and analysis on the donors and the telemarketing campaign itself.

Women's College Hospital Foundation

Women's College Hospital Foundation (WCHF) uses telemarketing software called Campus Call published by RuffaloCody. It tracks all its prospects in this application and the results of the phone call, either positive or negative. It asked JMG Solutions to create a software interface program that would convert the positive data (i.e., donation) to the fund-raising management system. Now on a daily basis, or any other time frame as the foundation chooses, donor and donation information can be electronically transferred to the fund-raising management system for tax receipt and report purposes.

The Internet

Now, in addition to name and address details, we are also able to capture the World Wide Web and e-mail addresses of donors and prospects. Companies and even some foundations now have established Web sites. At the same time, more not-for-profits are also developing Web sites, and many have organizational or staff e-mail addresses.

Many of today's charities are using e-mail addresses to keep donors up to date and to communicate with board members by sending them minutes of meetings and other bulletins. E-mail is quick and often immediate, depending on how often recepients check for messages. This method of communication can be more cost effective than using faxes, couriers, and regular mail.

E-commerce, the Internet, and the Database With e-commerce, the Internet is fast becoming a new solicitation vehicle. When a donation is made over the World Wide Web, that information is sent to someone for processing. Output from a web page could be programmed to create a file, which could be imported into the fund-raising management system. This would save time from having to manually enter the information into the system and would reduce errors. While the donor enters information on the Web site, the site could ensure that the correct information is entered into the standard format, thus ensuring accuracy and standardization.

Access Outside of the Office Some development professionals are spending more time outside of the office. They are increasingly using the Internet to access and print their donor information. More and more fund-raising management systems are allowing fund-raising professionals to access donor records and information via the Internet. The development officer logs onto the database just as if he or she were in the office. Doing so would allow the person to add notes, change an address, or print important information needed for an upcoming meeting.

An Unlimited Source of Information   As the number of Web sites is growing by the minute, so are the sources of information available to find out more about donors and prospects. Many Web sites offer free information; some require users to join as a member for no fee; others charge a nominal membership fee, some on a per-request basis; and others have more extensive detailed information at a higher access cost.

The Web provides information on people, companies, governments, and foundations not only in your own country but also internationally. Some international sites also contain details on prospects in your own country. You can find prospect addresses and their own specific sites or those that provide information on any number of prospects.

The Challenge   So much information is available for prospect research that it could become a black hole that absorbs all of our researcher's time and resources. The processes the fund-raiser puts in place must include the transfer of information into his or her database.

To date, legislation has been limited with regard to personal information, accountability, access, and data protection. Countries in Europe with their Data Protection Act are already looking into regulating the Internet. Not-for-profits have a responsibility to ensure that we are responsible and accountable to donors and those we are here to provide services for. Most of all, fund-raisers need to respect their wishes and keep an eye on what is reasonable in the directions we go from here.

The Internet has much to be explored, for both fund-raising from your own Web sites and prospect research. The challenge is to keep up on this vast and ever-changing world and to capture it all in our own database systems.

Conclusion

Technological changes have made databases more than inert objects. They are now sophisticated pieces of software that allow you to do more than just capture the name, address, and gift amount of a donor.

But organizations shouldn't get ahead of themselves with databases. While computerized databases can do sophisticated tasks, many organizations haven't mastered the basics of any database—paper or electronic—before they begin to use the full capabilities of new database systems. That's why this chapter began with a very clear outline of the basics of any database.

Once an organization has mastered the basics, it's time to turn your attention to more sophisticated uses of the database—whether that's linking to the Internet, using bar code scanning, or using the database to improve donor development.

Finally, using the database as a research tool is truly using the database as a holistic tool in fund-raising. Now the database can be used to take the direct-response fund-raising donors (who make smaller, more modest gifts) and move them to larger and larger gifts over their lifetime as supporters.

The databases of today and tomorrow will give nonprofit organizations the tools to almost step inside the head of their supporters. If the databases are set up correctly, fund-raisers will be able to understand donors' values and shifting life experiences, and understand them as people and donors. What every organization needs to understand is that technology is giving them the tools to get closer to their supporters—not farther away.

By mastering the ideas and examples in this chapter, any nonprofit organization will be able to better understand, secure, and keep its future donors.

New Media and Direct-Response Fund-Raising

JASON POTTS

Introduction

The term "new media" is a cover-all term that describes different data storage and transfer devices—the World Wide Web, e-mail, computer diskettes, DVDs, interactive television, touch-screen kiosks, and CD-ROMs. New media is playing an increasing part in direct-response fund-raising initiatives around the world. It is also making an increasing claim to be added to fund-raisers' armory of responsive media in its own right. Whether it is a diskette in a mail pack, a CD-ROM linking a specific target audience to a Web site, or a secure credit card donation facility promoted through a Web address on a direct-response television (DRTV) advertisement, new media is rapidly becoming credible responsive media (inquiries and donations) for fund-raisers worldwide.

The increasing availability of Web-ready devices, big investment from leading commercial brands, and the transformation of certain types of business through e-commerce are just some of the factors contributing to massive worldwide on-line audience growth. Unlike existing direct-response media, many of the rules are yet to be established, let alone tested. Yet the opportunities for fund-raisers are increasingly clear. This chapter looks at these opportunities and how some organizations around the world are beginning to take advantage of them. It is divided into five key areas:

1. New media—setting the scene for fund-raisers
2. Applying the tried and tested techniques of direct response to new media
3. Integrating new media components into existing initiatives
4. The impact of new media technologies on recruitment and supporter communications
5. A look at how new media technologies could develop over the next few years, with the possible impacts on not-for-profits

The fast-changing nature of new media means that anything printed on this subject has the danger of being out of date before the ink has had time to dry on the page. With this is mind, this chapter looks at general trends rather than specifics with some indicative nonprofit examples.

What Are New Media?

First, let's take a step back. "New media" is a cover-all term, which at its most basic level describes different data storage and transfer devices, as specified. The various devices are grouped together because they are comparatively new (most of the terms would have been unfamiliar to many a year or so ago) and because they all use the same basic language: digital. Because digital information can be transferred effortlessly through existing communications networks (satellite, cable, or the telephone) and can be viewed easily on differing output devices (TV, personal computer, a hybrid, mobile phone or indeed wristwatch), the convergence of new media is potentially the biggest advance in communications technology since movable type.

When one talks about new media and direct-response fund-raising today, one is talking mainly about the Web and e-mail. But that's not the new media of the future. The rapid convergence of this technology with existing networks—TV, telephone, and global intranets—means that the global information infrastructure, much vaunted in the writings of U.S. Vice President Al Gore, is becoming an increasing reality. What is called the Internet today will be a far more widely accessed global information channel in the not too distant future.

For fund-raisers, digital media offer new channels of communication with key audiences: prospects, supporters, partners, beneficiaries, or sponsors. These communication channels allow them to interact and respond as they choose and allows tracking in enough detail to treat them as individuals.

Clearly, the new media's ability to individualize fund-raising should be of interest to fund-raising practitioners worldwide, particularly as the cost of entry to some of these technologies is often not great. (For example, I've included the costs and capabilities for a screensaver for a nonprofit organization at the end of this chapter.) Also, the Web offers a level playing field in terms of audience reach to both big corporate brands and small nonprofits. In many cases creativity and ingenuity can go a long way toward maximizing a modest budget. (See Exhibit 5.1 and visit Greenpeace UK's Web site at www.greenpeace.org.uk. The area of the site

EXHIBIT 5.1   Greenpeace Web Site/Interactive Games

Used with permission from Greenpeace UK.

focusing on genetically modified food includes interactive games and competitions that are engaging, exciting, and not expensive.)

Setting the Scene   Tracking the growth of new media worldwide is far from an exact science, and a great deal of hyperbole has preceded actual fact. Audience figures vary from survey to survey, but the general consensus is one of massive growth in a very short space of time, growth that at the moment is showing no signs of slowing down. Quite the opposite, in fact.

Figures for usage and user demographics are changing as quickly as new media grow, diversify, and converge. According to Anne Leer of Financial Times Management in *Masters of the Wired World:*

- In five years the number of computers connected to the Internet has grown from 1.3 million to 37 million
- Traffic on the Web doubles every 100 days

- Content grows at a rate of 1.5 million pages per day and its size doubles every eight months

The ability to visit the Web on a TV set will undoubtedly add to this remarkable growth. TV penetration worldwide is far greater than PC penetration, and the cost of using an existing TV compared to investing in a Web-ready PC allows lower-income households access. Interactive TV is just beginning to deliver statistically meaningful audiences, as a percentage of the overall population, in the more developed economies. According to www.datamonitor.com, there will be an estimated 67 million interactive households across the United States and Europe by the year 2003, up from 10.3 million in 1998.

The Internet first developed within a particular demographic slice: young educated males, in a particular geographic location, the United States and Canada. Large worldwide growth, the increasing ease of access (there are around 3,000 Internet service providers in Europe alone), support infrastructures (24-hour help lines), and the commercialization of the Web for e-business (dot.coms continue to capitalize on the stock markets at incredible levels) have meant that all existing profiles are rapidly flattening. Trends for the millennium indicate:

- The rest of the world is catching up the United States and Canada as the major user base.
- Women are set to overtake men as the most represented gender.
- People over 50 are the fastest-growing audience (according to www.nua.com) and they are using new media: Dan Goldhar, the general manager of Fifty Plus Net (www.fifty-plus.net), a nonprofit organization that provides Internet community services to individuals over 50, presents some intriguing information about over-50 Net users.
- WebTV is the number-one access point for his 5,000 plus visitors. Over 50 percent of visitors get access that way, and the number is growing for over-50 users.
- There are two distant groups of seniors on-line. The first have low-end computers, often old machines given to them by kids or grandkids. The second group has jumped right over the computer and gotten on-line with WebTV.

A broad look at the on-line audience shows that the main users of the Web, e-mail, and digital TV are no longer college students and academics but instead businesses and individuals who fit more with existing not-for-profit supporter databases. The audience also consists of new younger people that not-for-profits traditionally have had difficulty reaching through more conventional communications channels.

New Media and the Techniques of Direct Response

Now that the scene has been set, let us begin by looking at how tried and tested techniques of direct response can be used to get results through new media. Simply putting a mail pack on-line or digitizing a TV ad and waiting for the donations to come flooding in has proved a frustrating experience for many nonprofit organizations.

By studying the lessons learned from years of direct mail and direct-response TV (DRTV) in the sector, by doing as much testing as possible (see Chapter 6), and by sticking to their off-line brand values, Amnesty International UK (www.amnesty.org.uk) was able to make a success of its fund-raising site.

Case Study—Amnesty International UK   The objective for the site was to learn as much as possible about fund-raising on-line and at the same time recruit supporters at a profit. When entering the support area of the site from the home page, the visitor was given one of three randomly generated appeals. These test both creative and technological sophistication. Creatively:

- Appeal 1 (see Exhibit 5.2) tells a good news story of an individual released from prison because of the letters received by Amnesty supporters worldwide.
- Appeal 2 (see Exhibit 5.3) invites the visitor to click on a series of yes/no boxes to answer questions (it might be compared to a questionnaire mailing) such as, have you ever read a book? or would you defend your family?
- Appeal 3 (see Exhibit 5.4) is very hard hitting and uses animation and sound to bring to life the story of Maria, imprisoned and brutally tortured by an oppressive regime

As in all good fund-raising, these were real stories about real people. And the way to give was made very simple; on two of the screens the phrase "click the candle (the Amnesty logo) to help" was prominent.

EXHIBIT 5.2   Amnesty International Letters

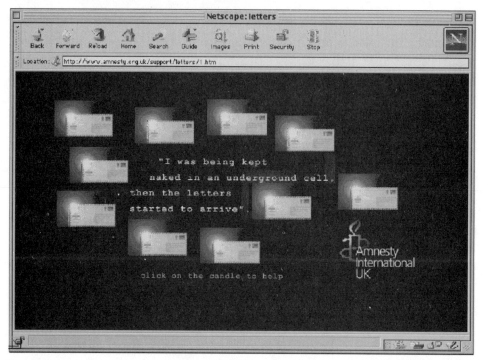

Used with permission from Amnesty International UK.

EXHIBIT 5.3   Amnesty International Question Box

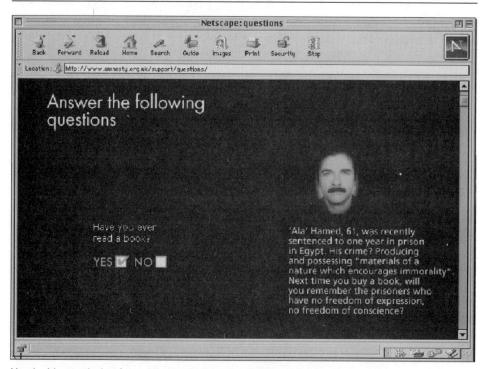

Used with permission from Amnesty International UK.

EXHIBIT 5.4   Amnesty International Maria Story

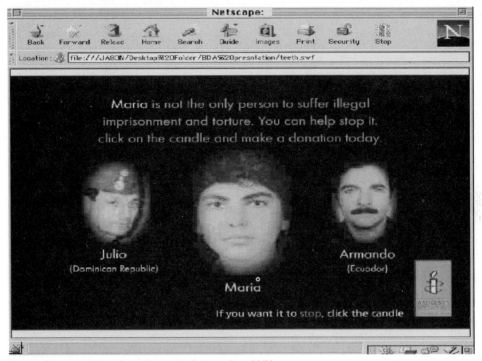

Used with permission from Amnesty International UK.

The appeals also tested Web technology. At one end of the scale the appeals were simple HTML pages; at the other end, they were complicated JavaScript animation with accompanying sound files. So as not to disappoint prospective donors, the site sensed what type of browser each visitor had and served up only that appeal that the browser could view. (I'll explain more about this later.)

With such a new medium, it was necessary to test as much as possible to lay the groundwork for what works and what doesn't for future on-line activities. And so, membership was tested against one-time donations, and two different reply forms were created and were served up randomly from each appeal. (See Exhibits 5.5a and 5.5b). This area of the site also featured a questionnaire to capture more qualitative data about site visitors.

After six months the site produced a return on investment of 1 to 1.8. This favorable quick return on investment is set against a backdrop of the vast majority of organizations in the United Kingdom which are unable to make such recruitment through other forms of advertising cost effective.

EXHIBIT 5.5A   Amnesty International UK Membership Form

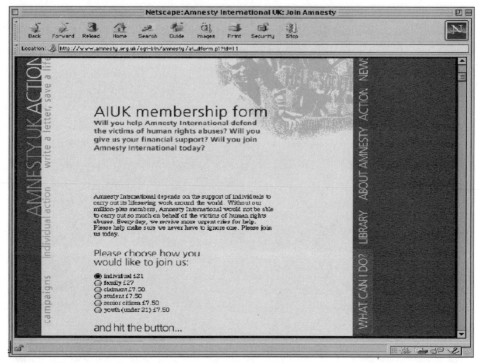

Used with permission from Amnesty International UK.

EXHIBIT 5.5B   Amnesty International UK Donation Form

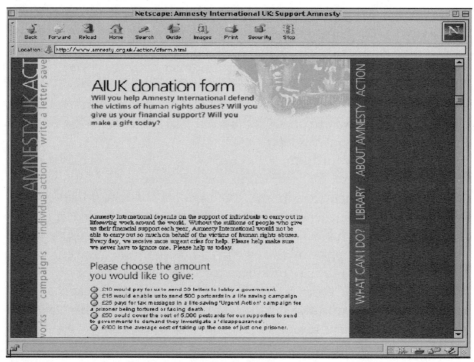

Used with permission from Amnesty International UK.

In addition, the costs of recruiting a new supporter through cold mail can cost anywhere between £3 to £10. A total number of new members recruited of 846 shows that the medium has become a viable alternative to conventional channels. The total number of donations (regular, ad hoc, or with membership subscription) was 101. In addition, over 600 questionnaires were returned.

Perhaps not surprisingly, membership worked better than one-time donations. Amnesty is, after all, a membership organization. Appeal 2, the interactive one, and the multimedia appeal (3) outperformed the more static appeal (1).

Adding New Media to the Mix

Integrating new media into a fund-raising campaign can open up new audiences and facilitate responses that might otherwise have gotten away. What follows are several examples of not-for-profits that are already adding new media elements to their fund-raising campaigns.

Case Study—Press Advertising

Greenpeace UK—True Food Campaign   The aim of the campaign was to publicize Greenpeace's call to ban genetically modified foods and promote organically grown alternatives. The campaign saw Greenpeace UK adding a Web site (see Exhibit 5.6) and e-mail communications program to a national press campaign (see Exhibit 5.7). Time was very much of the essence to make the most of the surrounding news media coverage about genetically modified foods. The direct-response media chosen needed to be rapidly enabled. The day after the issue became front-page news in most U.K. broadsheets, the press advertisements appeared and the Web site was launched.

The press advertisements allowed respondents to request more information through the post or directed those with Internet access to a Web site that was regularly updated with new campaign developments. The site was created specifically for this activity and taken off-line afterward. Once on-line, visitors were able to make a donation or request more information about the issues via post or e-mail. Not surprisingly, most opted for e-mail.

The press activity stimulated traffic on the Web site while offering site visitors an e-mail communication option stimulated response. From a

EXHIBIT 5.6   Greenpeace UK Web Site

Used with permission from Greenpeace UK.

standing start, as the site had no existing traffic, 600 new names with e-mail addresses were generated.

The direct mail pack sent to 100,000 Greenpeace members generated £75,000,[1] and the entire activity including phone, Web, and press inserts generated 8,000 requests for more information. With such a fast-moving campaign, Greenpeace learned that the more flexible response mechanisms of e-mail and telemarketing were far more effective than traditional supporter communications channels.

Case Study—DRTV

Comic Relief—Red Nose Day 1999   Red Nose Day 1999 was called the "record breaker," in the fund-raising sense, the eight-hour live telethon on

---

[1]Throughout this chapter one British pound equals approximately $1.50 U.S. dollars.

EXHIBIT 5.7   Greenpeace Press Campaign "Leave It Out Tony!"

Genetically engineered foods are, well, look, you know, kind of terrific, aren't they?

Leave it out Tony!

To find out more about the genetic food fiasco and what the alternatives are, call free on 0800 269 065 or visit www.greenpeace.org.uk/truefood

GREENPEACE

Used with permission from Greenpeace UK.

national TV offered great exposure to a large audience. The Web site address, www.rednoseday.org.uk and www.rednoseday.beeb.com was repeated at regular intervals during the TV show (see Exhibit 5.8). To attract a global audience, the show was Webcast live. The site opened up a new fund-raising route for Comic Relief, and approximately 2 percent of all donations were made via the Web on the night of the appeal. Almost 14,000 donations came in from all over the world; 13,508 donations were

EXHIBIT 5.8   Comic Relief/Red Nose Day

Used with permission from Comic Relief.

in British sterling; 83 in U.S. dollars; 11 in Australian dollars; nine in Canadian dollars, 134 in euros; and 107 in Irish punts.

Overall, 5 million "click throughs" or page impressions were served with nearly 700,000 visits over a seven-week period. The sites generated nearly 9,000 extra e-mail addresses.

One of the biggest challenges for nonprofits using new media will be their e-mail solicitations. This little-understood area needs further experimentation.

New Media as a Stand-Alone Direct Response Tool

Fund-raisers around the world such as Amnesty International are also finding that digital media can be used as a relatively low-cost recruitment and retention medium in its own right. Recruitment is all about attracting as many people as possible to a Web site and converting them into donors or members, or at least collecting e-mail addresses for future communications.

Several organizations have found that once visitors have been attracted to a site, allowing them to join e-mail mailing lists or enter member-only areas are good ways of strengthening their commitment to a cause.

Recruitment Methods

Search Engines/On-line Public Relations   With 70 percent of Web visitors beginning on-line sessions by visiting a search engine, the art of positioning a site prominently on these listings is worth investment. Few other direct-response media provide such low-cost access to such a vast global audience. Key words and phrases to describe an organization and its work need to be chosen carefully. Finding an individual or company to do the registration and meta-tags (ways of submitting key words to search engines to ensure a high ranking) also should be done very carefully. Organizations serious about their on-line presence should not allow well-meaning amateurs to do these jobs.

Check the organization's positioning on search engine listings, as it will change. Listings can be checked by visiting www.rankthis.com. Interestingly, for the word "environment" on Yahoo! does not list Greenpeace in the top 200. It's also important to note that time lines vary with each search engine. However, allow approximately six weeks for your organization's listing on a search engine to appear.

Many larger organizations suffer from too many site listings, either from regional or country offices or from well-meaning supporters putting up a site in the belief they are doing the organization in question a good turn. For example, searching for the Red Cross on Lycos, a typical search engine, produces over 88,000 listings, the first of which mentions Elizabeth Dole leaving the Red Cross. No disrespect to Mrs. Dole, but this is perhaps not the best way to introduce a potential supporter to a global organization. This problem is certainly not unusual. Clearly it is every bit as important to protect a brand image on-line as in off-line direct response materials. Providing prospects with the easiest path possible to finding and joining an organization on-line is crucial.

Other low-cost promotional opportunities exist through on-line public relations, organizing reciprocal links with high-traffic sites, getting links on listings and What's Hot sites, and also informing likely news groups. Links can generate enormous traffic. Greenpeace International currently has over 28,500 sites linked to www.greenpeace.org, and, not surprisingly, it has one of the most visited sites in the nonprofit sector.

To find out who is linked to a site, visit www.altavista.com and type link: followed by the web address (i.e., link: www.greenpeace.org). This will return a list of all sites linked to a site. Viewers may well be surprised.

Banner Advertising   Banner advertising can be described most simply as a link on a third-party site that is designed to grab visitors' attention and take them to another site. As with all direct-response media, the key is to place a banner advertisement on a site that has a large percentage of the target market as regular visitors (at the right price). Click-through rates from banners are usually reckoned to be between 0.5 to 5 percent. The percentage of people who will then request more information or donate is no more than 1 to 5 percent.

From these statistics, it is plain to see that banner advertising, like most marketing, is very much a numbers game. The good news for not-for-profits looking to get people to their Web site is that the cost of banner advertising is not prohibitive. For most high-traffic sites a cost of £25 to £30 per 1,000 views is not uncommon. Testing is very economical because many high-traffic sites will allow potential users to pay for several thousand views to get an idea of how the banners are performing and what revenue or inquiries are being generated. Based on results, it is possible to revise the banner, concentrate further views on the most successful areas of the site, change the ask, or look for another host site with a different audience profile.

For forward-thinking fund-raisers, opportunities exist to negotiate good banner deals with high-traffic sites or by putting banners on existing corporate sponsors' sites. Many blue-chip companies have many site visitors and probably a global intranet. Having a banner on the intranet, which can link to the Web, of a large global corporate presents enormous opportunity for interoffice competitive fund-raising challenges. It is also a low-cost way to keep donors informed of how much they have raised and how this money has been put to good use.

Making Effective Banners

Studies conducted by Milward Brown Interactive in 1999 found the following five facts about banners that is directly applicable to any nonprofit organization:

1. Multimedia banners are more likely to be noticed by visitors than standard, static GIF banners.
2. Multimedia banners increased customers' positive perception of a branded product over static GIF banners.
3. Click-through rates increased from 50 to 400 percent with multimedia banners.
4. Multimedia banners had a positive impact on those consumers who were ready to buy right away (as well as those who weren't ready to buy at that moment but could be influenced positively for a possible future purchase).
5. Brand recall was improved with multimedia banners over static banners.

The multimedia banners were built using FLASH and JAVA script animation software tools. Nonprofit organizations should pay only $150 to $200 for an animated banner. Yehoshua Bendah, a programmer and Internet consultant for Hewitt and Johnston Consultants, offers the following advice for creating effective banners:

- Make it interesting enough so that there is some *mystery* in it, so people will be attracted to read them, and click.
- If possible, at least 3 shifts (panels), and even if it can remain small enough in size—for all intents and purposes you can build a few teasers one on top of one another leading to the demand for an action.
- Organizations should tantalize the reader into clicking on the banner to "find something out" or make a difference.
- These days people are beginning to associate banners with an intrusive commercialism, so anyway the banner can make it clear that this a nonprofit message, the better without losing the direct response necessity of capturing someone's interest to act

A Banner Case Study

Besides targeting banners by host site visitor profile, most search engines will also allow banners triggered by the search for key words. For example, animal charities might want a banner to appear when someone searches for the words "cat" or "dog."

Recently the National Abortion Rights Action League (NARAL) tested banner ads with juno.com. (Juno provides Internet services for over 7 million Americans.) When a prospective supporter clicked on the NARAL banner, a survey popped up. NARAL was out to build an on-line database of activists. Another organization might have had a click take someone to a donation page. In their case, NARAL got the following results:

- It was able to select 130,000 Juno members who fit a favorable demographic for NARAL.
- Those 130,000 members saw a NARAL banner that asked them to get involved in abortion rights.
- When they clicked on the banner, up popped a survey.
- Twenty-five thousand of these individuals actually filled out a survey that popped up after the banner was clicked.
- Of these, 15,000 gave home and e-mail addresses.
- These 15,000 were emailed and asked to take an action (e.g., send an e-mail).
- Of these 15,000, 3,000 took an action on-line or made a donation.

In a very short time, NARAL built a database of 15,000 prospective supporters. This banner case study should remind every nonprofit organization that banner ads can help you think big: Imagine finding 15,000 new supporters in a week—or even one day. The new media have accelerated a nonprofit's time line to build a database of like-minded people.

What Do to After You've Got the E-Mail Addresses

Moveon.org is a political reform organization that began as a grass-roots movement to force U.S. federal politicians to leave the Clinton sex scandal behind and get on to an agenda focused on issues. Their site at www.moveon.org collected 500,000 on-line signatures and received 25,000 on-line pledges, all of it to get Congress and the Senate to move on from impeachment.

Moveon.org decided not to approach these pledgers to actually give a gift. After about a six-month delay, the organization sent out 16,000 e-mails. Recipients of the e-mail could visit a site that showed the politicians who backed Clinton's impeachment process, and they could make an immediate on-line gift. The organization made $250,000 U.S. in just five days on-line. The average gift was $10, and 92 percent of gifts were under $50. While this example shows that organizations can wait to e-mail prospective supporters, Yahoo has found that almost 50 percent of e-mail addresses change in one year, so don't wait too long.

The Environmental Defense Fund collected 125,000 e-mail addresses for its action-focused e-mail newsletter. It got 50,000 e-mail addresses from a juno.com promotion (similar to NARAL), then send an e-mail newsletter every three weeks to on-line newsletter subscribers. Of the 125,000 people asked for money, 0.3 percent responded to e-mail by going to the on-line giving form, and 75 percent of those individuals gave on-line.[2]

NSPCC Virtual Collecting Tin As part of the Full Stop initiative, a campaign launched in 1999 to end child abuse forever, the NSPCC developed an on-line icon, the Virtual Collecting Tin (VCT). This allowed corporate sponsors to visit a Web address (www.nspcc.org.uk/vct/hosts) (see Exhibit 5.9), and pick up a banner to put on their site. The campaign was to continue over the course of 1999 and 2000, so it was important to make the process of putting the banner on a host site as simple and automated as possible.

---

[2]All of the above banner and e-mail results come from Nick Allen's presentation at the DMA Conference in Toronto, November 1999.

EXHIBIT 5.9   NSPCC Virtual Collecting Tin

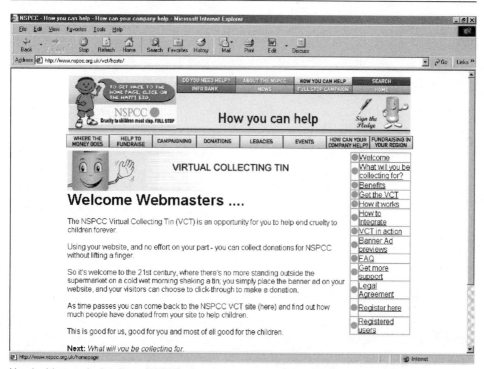

Used with permission from NSPCC.

Prospective hosts were approached through the NSPCC's existing corporate supporters, and an on-line public relations campaign was mounted to approach various selected high-traffic sites.

True to conventional direct-response logic, various aspects of the campaign were tested. Three different types of banners (see Exhibits 5.10, 5.11, 5.12) were produced with different creative approaches. Three different appeals were created to present to the visitors once they had clicked through to the NSPCC site. The data from these tests were automatically logged and fed into a database that had an on-line password-protected viewing area.

The NSPCC site was populated with the VCT image of the Virtual Collecting Tin (see Exhibit 5.13). Various categories of visitor were identified and given appropriate content based on what the site knew about them. For example, those who had already made a donation were not given an appeal again when they clicked on the VCT but were taken straight through to the donation option page. Because of some nervousness in

EXHIBIT 5.10   NSPCC VCT "Don't Close Your Eyes to Child Abuse"

Used with permission from NSPCC.

EXHIBIT 5.11   NSPCC VCT "Cruelty to Children Must Stop. Full Stop."

Used with permission from NSPCC.

EXHIBIT 5.12   NSPCC VCT "It's 'Virtually' Here . . ."

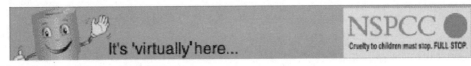

Used with permission from NSPCC.

EXHIBIT 5.13   NSPCC VCT "Click Here to Make a Donation"

CLICK HERE TO
MAKE A DONATION.

Used with permission from NSPCC.

Europe about on-line secure credit card transactions, visitors were given the option of secure credit card or print, post, or fax donations.

The early results show that from the big-traffic sites, many people can be directed to the organization's site and encouraged to get involved with the campaign. So far, the VCT has over 70 host sites, 10,725 people have clicked through to the NSPCC donation area, 125 on-line donations have been made, 244 print and post donation forms have been requested, and 477 requests for more information have been logged.

On-line Emergency Appeals   The urgent nature of the Web as a communications medium is giving fund-raisers around the world involved with disaster relief organizations a new channel through which to communicate instantly to potential and existing supporters. The crisis in Kosovo set the on-line cash registers ringing on both sides of the Atlantic. In the United States on-line fund-raising makes up a significant percentage of monies raised in emergency situations;

Organization	Total revenue	On-line total	On-line%
Oxfam America	$ 300,000	$ 43,000	14 %
Save the Children	$ 125,000	$ 40,000	32 %
American Red Cross	$6,100,000	$545,000	8.9%

The American Red Cross, perhaps the most successful on-line fund-raising organization in the world, is reported to have raised over $9 million in Web donations in 1999. Along with larger and larger gift totals for emergency appeals, organizations are building larger e-mail databases. The American Red Cross built a database of over 15,000 individuals during the Kosovo crisis. The fund-raising potential of this e-mail database is exciting.

In the United Kingdom, the Charities Aid Foundation received over £30,000 in less than a month in on-line donations through its CharityCard Web site (www.charitycard.org) in support of Kosovan refugees. This took the total donated through the site since its launch just one year earlier to £170,000.

CD-ROMs   CD-ROMs are a good way to target a specific audience and provide them with lots of high-quality, multimedia information. They also can be used to link audiences to an organization's Web site. The problem is that CD-ROMs often are prohibitively expensive to produce without a guaranteed return on investment. However, low-cost alternatives exist to producing a CD-ROM. One is putting material on other CDs that are already being distributed to likely target audiences. Amnesty International, Greenpeace, and Great Ormond Street Children's Hospital were all able to put information on a CD-ROM, which goes to every final-year college and university student in the United Kingdom. The main function of the disk is to enable students to search through a large database of prospective employers. Among this career-matching facility are other offers and promotions.

The three charities put on some simple information and several pieces of video to appeal to this audience and make them aware of the work they do. The students were then able to link to the organizations' Web sites to find out more, join, or volunteer. This was inexpensive and in this case very well targeted. Linked to competitions or interactive content, this kind of activity can stimulate interest from younger age groups that are not traditionally known for their philanthropic nature.

Cold E-mail   Cold e-mail, or "spamming," has created mixed results for not-for-profits. Organizations that have attempted large-scale mailings have run into severe problems. A European-based landmine charity had so many complaints after sending out an unsolicited e-mail that its service provider pulled the plug on its account. Oxfam in the United Kingdom began and then aborted e-mail recruitment tests due to adverse initial reactions.

A good example of what *not* to do comes from the Children's Hunger Fund, which bought one million e-mail names for $700 and sent one million e-mail messages out as part of a Kosovo appeal. It raised a measly $1,600 but received a pile of negative reactions including warnings from two U.S. State attorneys general. An antispammer activist contacted the fund's Internet service provider to pressure it to not allow that kind of mass e-mail solicitation to be sent out again.

Organizations using more targeting are having more success. For example, the University of Maryland generated $100,000. The audience it mailed belonged to news groups that discussed the particular medical issues the university was asking readers to support. The equivalent of on-line member-get-member schemes have also proved popular. Tearfund (a U.K.-based development agency) invited supporters visiting the site to send e-mail postcards to their friends directing them to the site to pick up a message and find out more.

With 18 percent response levels currently being generated from unpersonalized e-mail in the commercial sector according to Forrester, a marketing research company, not-for-profits shouldn't give up but should wait for the right moment and the right targeted audience to come along.

Retention Methods In addition to the straightforward recruitment of new supporters, new media also offer fund-raisers the opportunity to build relationships with donors or supporters.

Ken Burnett, a fund-raising guru in the United Kingdom, emphasizes something called relationship fund-raising.[3] Relationship fund-raising preaches a donor-based focus to the business of fund-raising. This donor focus holds true as much for this direct-response medium as any other. Indeed, the automated segmentation and data storage capacity of the backend technologies underpinning a database-driven site allow fund-raisers to get closer than ever before to genuine two-way dialogues built on supporter choice.

The nature of digital communication allows the storage of a great deal of information that can be pulled into predesigned templates easily. Digital tools also allow site visitors to choose the information they require and customize and personalize their information. The next time they return to the site digital tools (software & hardware) will remember their preferences and exhibit a personalize approach for them. (See Exhibit 5.14a–g).

---

[3]Ken's books, *Friends For Life: Relationship Fundraising in Practice* and *Relationship Fundraising: A Donor-Based Approach to the Business of Raising Money,* are both available from White-lion Press.

EXHIBIT 5.14A–G   Database-Driven Web Sites—The Theory

Database-driven Web Sites-
The Theory

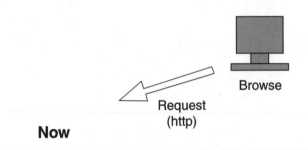

**Request
(http)**

Browse

(a)   **Now**

Database-driven Web Sites-
The Theory

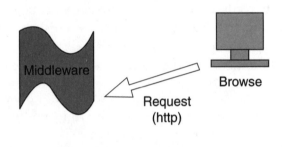

Middleware

Browse

**Request
(http)**

(b)   **Now**

Database-driven Web Sites-
The Theory

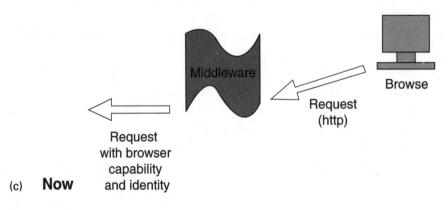

Middleware

Browse

**Request
(http)**

**Request
with browser
capability
and identity**

(c)   **Now**

Used with permission from Burnett & Associates.

EXHIBIT 5.14A–G   Continued

Database-driven Web Sites- The Theory

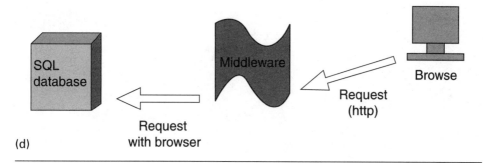

(d)

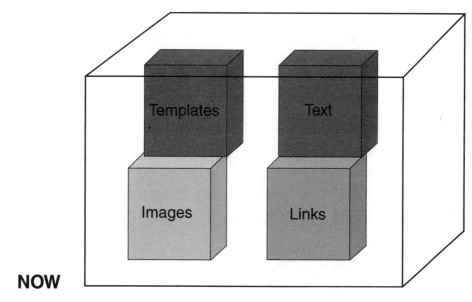

NOW

(e)

EXHIBIT 5.14A–G   Continued

Database-driven Web Sites-
The Theory

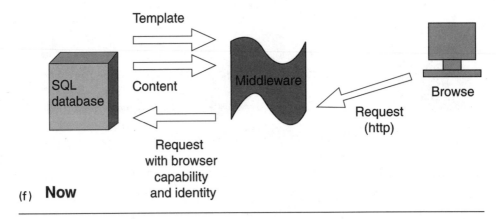

(f) **Now**

Database-driven Web Sites-
The Theory

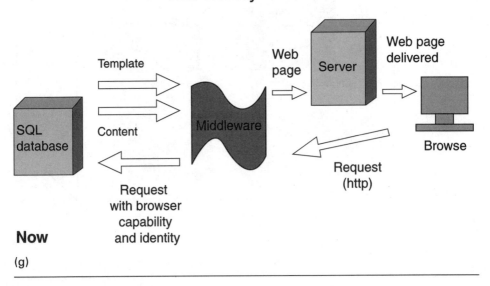

Now

(g)

The above exhibits show how database technology differs from static HTML Web site production.

Effectively, all site visitors could have their own individual home page based on only the content in which they are interested. Knowing what it is that interests an individual about a cause is clearly very valuable knowledge for a fund-raiser in terms of targeting future correspondence of all kinds and maximizing the impact of any ask.

Add to this push technology, where an e-mail can be generated automatically whenever a particular area of the site in which a supporter has shown an interest is updated, and it is easy to see how inexpensive relationships can be managed effectively and successfully.

The site of a U.K.-based development charity, Tearfund (see Exhibits 5.15 and 5.16), employs just such a database-driven system. It uses a product called Microsoft SiteServer to enable some of the backend data tracking and e-mail list servers. On arriving at the home page, visitors are presented with a series of buttons that allow them to make choices about the content they wish to see. Tearfund works in many places all over the world, and visitors are allowed to select countries that interest them most. The site does this automatically by tracking viewers' behavior over time and then relegating areas of less interest to lower levels of navigation.

EXHIBIT 5.15   Tearfund "Your Profile"

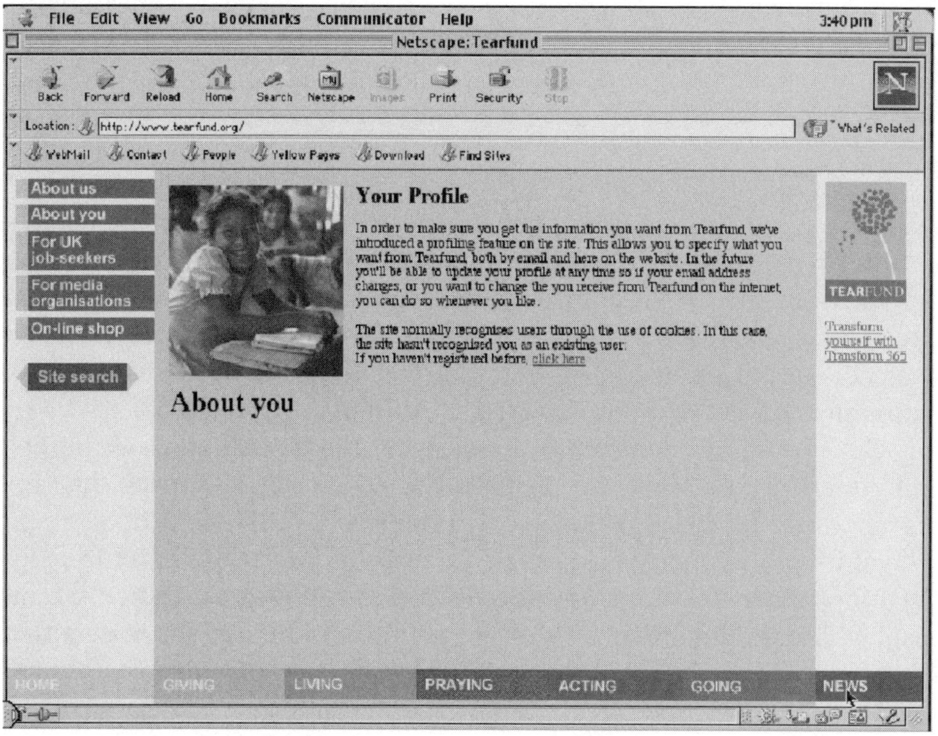

Used with permission from Tearfund.

EXHIBIT 5.16   Tearfund "Thanks for Registering"

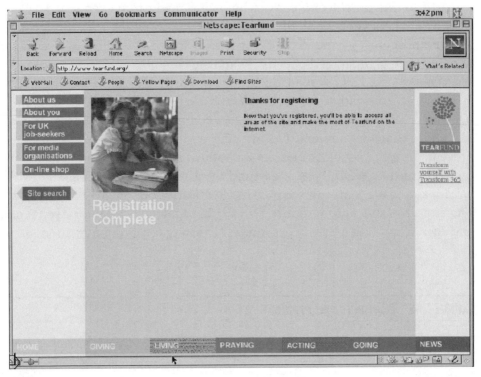

Used with permission from Tearfund.

During the Kosovo crisis, the site raised over £14,000 in under two weeks by e-mailing 3,000 warm supporters, names that the site had collected over time. In keeping with other on-line giving trends, the fund received several healthy donations of £1,000 as part of that total. Tearfund was able to put up an appeal within a day and send out e-mails asking supporters to visit the site and make a donation.

Greenpeace Sweden employs a different model with its 3,000 on-line supporters. In the same way that regular giving schemes bring the supporter closer to the organization, Greenpeace Sweden uses its site and e-mail to give supporters access to all kinds of information and to regularly update them about news items affecting the organization's campaigns. It uses the immediacy of the medium to inform supporters that Greenpeace might be appearing on the news that evening and can present its side of the issue and offer background information.

Conclusion: New Media and Direct Response Tomorrow

Some of the key ways that not-for-profits around the world are beginning to use new media as a direct-response medium have been outlined. Of course, there are many other ways; lotteries, auctions, treasure hunts, and on-line petitions, to name but a few.

Several factors are stimulating the environment of opportunity. Politicians and chief executives across the globe are investing time and, more important, money in making the digital future a reality. Major investments include equipping educational institutions and public facilities (such as libraries) as well as the home user market and local government initiatives to empower the information poor. Technological advances are creating further openings:

- Moore's Law dictates that computing power will double while its cost will half over a 12- to 18-month period for the foreseeable future, most likely spelling an end to the user's wait experience on the World Wide Web.
- Interactive TV in many homes will unlock a larger audience, with a demographic profile more representative of society as a whole.
- Low-level communication satellites will allow access from any point on the globe.

Increasingly it is not the technology, the audience, or the resources that are holding organizations back but the *imagination*. So, where could fundraisers go with a little imagination? Here are some possible ways that new media could help with both individual initiatives and supporter lifetime values:

- *Digital interactive TV:* The massive proliferation of channels will allow not-for-profits to provide programming or "documercials." The ability of viewers to jump from this programming to a Web site to make an instant donation has obvious benefits.

- *Communications:* The ability to share digital information, both internally and externally. A new media office will draw information in digitally from the field and turn it into material for supporters and the general public by wired editors. Furthermore, it will be checked at a senior level and posted to a Web site within a matter of hours or sent as an e-mail report to those supporters who have given to that scheme or particular fund-raising initiative in the past.

- *Revolutionizing volunteering.* The new media will empower retired supporters such as teachers or engineers to communicate with an organization's partners or beneficiaries either locally or globally, to offer help and advice, improving both the services the organization offers and the bond between the organization and that supporter.

- *Creating on-line advocates.* Supporters will be able to communicate with each other, perhaps sharing information on an event they have recently taken part in, such as a bike ride or marathon. It is often at this grass-roots level that the best fund-raising stories are found.

- *Education:* Curriculum-based on-line educational materials to familiarize a younger audience with a cause can be combined with school fund-raising initiatives or volunteering.

- *Twinning.* Facilitating fund-raising initiatives in one area for beneficiaries in another and using the technology to put donors directly in touch with the people or project they are supporting.

- *E-mail communications programs.* These include strategies for allowing donors access to as much or as little information about an organization as required, coupled with the use of push technologies to maximize the use of automated information distribution and concentrate on one-to-one communications for key relationship-building customer services issues.

- *The daily me:* Allows increasingly busy supporters to download key updates (top-line topical information) from a site to their desktops or handheld devices, where the information can be read at their own convenience. Syndicating information through other content providers would give reach beyond existing on-line supporters.

- *Subscription services.* For those organizations that complete research or who develop technology or information (publication) that has a commercial value, on-line subscription services provide an easy, low-cost distribution channel.

- *Portals:* A portal is a definitive site on a particular subject area. For example, an environmental organization might develop a portal that would contain definitive content, services, and e-commerce around that environmental issue.

- *Selling third-party advertising:* This is a common aim for current high-traffic sites, but if the Internet makes the transition to a televisional broadcast medium, those on-line broadcasters with large or well-targeted audiences will be able to sell conventional TV commercials between their programming.

This list should provide food for thought for future planning. Clearly future-gazing has no guarantees, but many of these suggestions seem logical outgrowths of increased digital communications development.

In conclusion, new media applications are today beginning to produce results for fund-raisers worldwide. The way the new media are growing and are set to develop should offer further encouragement. But competition for audience is fierce, and consumer expectations from both a content and a customer service perspective are high. Failure to investigate these new fund-raising channels and to explore the low-cost supporter communications opportunities the new media provide would be a big mistake for not-for-profits.

APPENDIX A: Low Cost of Staying Top of Mind through a Screensaver

A screensaver can be a very effective, low-cost piece of new media for a nonprofit organization. A wide range of nonprofit organizations have created screensavers that can be downloaded from a Web site and/or can be sent on a diskette to a supporter.

A screensaver can use graphics, animation, and sound to communicate a mission and mandate through new media. For fund-raisers, giving messages in screensavers would be ideal.

What follows are some standard points in creating a screensaver. Creating one with the listed functionality should cost approximately $2,500 U.S. Imagine spending $2,500 and having thousands of supporters putting your screensaver on their computers. Every time their computers are inactive, the message will be scrolling across their screens. Now that's top of mind!

A new media nonprofit screensaver should include:

- PC and Mac versions of screensaver up to approximately 4 MB
- Compatibility: Windows 3.1, 95, 98, NT
- The nonprofit should send the supplier raw images in digital format (pict, PCX, PhotoShop, GID, JPG, whatever) at highest possible resolution.
- Nonprofit corporate logos or images for the icon and control panel should be included, as well as copyright notice and/or disclaimers.
- The supplier should reproduce as closely as possible the look and feel of the nonprofit organization's brand.
- The supplier should work with the nonprofit to provide additional creative/conceptual value to the screensaver. It should not be a static new media product. It needs to make supporters sit up and notice what's on their screen. It should be pleasing to look at. Ideally, it should be passed on from supporter to family and friends.
- The supplier needs to include bug testing.
- The supplier needs to provide an installation copy for Web site, plus troubleshooting copy.
- The supplier should work with the nonprofit to link a direct response function with the screensaver. For example, supporters might get the opportunity to download the screensaver only if they fill out an on-line survey.

APPENDIX B: *Interview with Graham Knope*

Graham Knope is president of Eagle-Com Inc., the company thought of as the premiere DRTV fund-raising firm. Its clients include Amnesty International, Greenepace USA, World Vision, and many others.

What Is DRTV?

DRTV, or direct-response television, are TV shows, often hosted by celebrities, that run for 15, 30, or 60 minutes on TV stations across North America. Viewers see a series of stories that provide an emotional explanation of the nonprofit's good work and ask them to pick up the phone and make a monthly gift right away.

Is This a New Area of Fund-Raising?

This is a fairly new vehicle for fund-raising, and it's only been around for approximately 20 years. World Vision was the earliest practitioner and Christian Children's Fund came thereafter.

This is a rather small market right now. Our firm, Eagle-Com, has 10 to 15 clients who use long-run DRTV fund-raising programming and on top of that there are only up to 10 others across North America who use it.

Statistics show that North Americans are watching more television. It's true that they are watching less network television, but they are watching more television overall (when you include their specialty channel watching).

The fragmentation of the television marketplace (with cable, satellite, etc.) means it's harder to reach your target audience.

With DRTV, I believe there has been an initial upsurge of demand from nonprofits wanting to make DRTV programming. As with any new product in the marketplace, there is an upward pressure on the demand curve. We get calls from more nonprofits who want to try DRTV, but we're just not able to meet the demand.

But that's a good thing because I think there is a slight bandwagon effect with this new fund-raising product. Everyone wants to get in but I really think there are a number of organizations who really can't make this kind of fund-raising work for their organization.

While I don't think the North American DRTV marketplace can hold 50 charities running their fund-raising programs across all marketplaces, I do think there is a place for more DRTV programming that is more targeted. The Breast Cancer Foundation may create a woman and breast cancer show that plays only on the Women's Television Network (a cable specialty channel). The show would reach a special market and would more than likely be a less expensive show.

So What's It Cost?

Costs are so variable, but it's important to know that there is considerable initial (and continuing) investment for considerable long term results. This is not a short-term endeavor. This is investing in a medium that can find you very loyal, very valuable monthly donors.

For a 30- to 60-minute show, a nonprofit organization can and should spend approximately $250,000 to $400,000. Then there is the cost of buying media time on TV stations to broadcast the show. Generally, you don't want to spend less on media buying than you did on producing the show. You want to show the programming to as many citizens as possible to build your monthly donor file as quickly as possible. The larger the media investment, the faster the return on investment.

It's most often a mistake to try to amortize the cost of producing the show by spending less on the media buys and relying on a smaller number of monthly donors to eventually pay for the cost of the show.

It generally takes 12 to 24 months for a show to pay for the initial investment of creating the show. Some nonprofit organizations break even in the first year, some break even in year two—it depends on the push to acquire monthly donors.

Are Celebrities Important?

We think they are vital. We want people to stop channel surfing when they come upon a nonprofit's DRTV show, and celebrities do that better than anything else.

When choosing a celebrity, make sure they add a perceived credibility to the show. For Amnesty International Canada, their use of Martin Sheen has paid off handsomely. He's a respected campaigner on human rights already, but currently he's the star of a hit TV show *The West Wing*. The use of his celebrity has increased the channel-stopping power of the show and made it incredibly profitable to Amnesty International Canada.

What Kind of Nonprofit Can Be Successful with DRTV?

I always ask a nonprofit to take the following test to determine whether they'd be appropriate for long-term TV fund-raising programming:

- Are you well recognized?
- Are you perceived to be highly reputable?
- Does your product (mission, those you help, etc.) show well on TV?
- Will your stories make good TV?
- Do you have emotional products and stories that pull for the mass market?
- Do you have a fund-raising program that is mature enough to have the experience and systems in place to take care of monthly donors for a long-term relationship? *This is vital because DTRV will fail on one-time donations!* It needs to capture monthly donors.
- Do you have a cause that relates itself to a monthly giving product? For example, child sponsorship lends itself to a monthly donation, but it's difficult to get donors to give a monthly gift for medical research. I don't believe it's impossible for health charities to raise money with DRTV (just look at St. Jude's Children's Research Hospital), but their monthly product must be carefully crafted to be as effective as possible.

A good example of a nonprofit that meets all of these criteria is the Toronto Humane Society. They've been so successful that their TV-acquired monthly supporters are the largest source of revenue for the organization. And remember, this is a single-building nonprofit in Toronto. It's not a national charity or even regional. It exists on just one street, in one city. Yet it is very successful at running one-hour TV fund-raising programs.

What Are the Bechmarks for Success?

With DRTV there are four essential indicators for success or failure. They are:

1. *The cost per lead.* This can vary tremendously from nonprofit to non-profit organization. Those nonprofits who've been in DRTV the

longest (the child sponsorship organizations) know the long-term value of their donors very well and therefore have a more elastic cost per lead. They can confidently spend more to find that donor than some other organizations because they know exactly the long-term return from that lead.

For the more mature DRTV programs, the cost per lead is somewhere around $100 per lead and approximately $200 for committed donor (someone who's signed on the dotted line). This may seem like a lot, but you've got to remember that the Long Term Value of a Donor (LTV) for these donors is over $2,000 (see Chapter 7's discussion on calculating LTV's).

However, for some other nonprofit organizations, their cost per lead is less expensive with a cost per lead of approximately $40 per lead to $150 per committed donor.

The fulfillment rate of leads is in 40 to 60 percent range.

The retention rates are anywhere from 75 to 85 percent a year.

DRTV is a mass marketing device. In many ways it is the least precise of the fund-raising mediums. It's true we want to be where the best donors are to be found, but for the most part we must rely on the whim of TV stations across North America. They decide when our kind of programming is allowed on air, and then we have to fit into their programming slots.

Without a doubt the best time for us to put on DRTV programming is daytime—during weekends and weekdays. Prime time is too expensive for nonprofits to afford, but that's not the time we'd want to be on the air anyway.

We want to be broadcasting into the home when there is more calm in the day—a time that allows for reflection and concern in people's lives. In the morning, people are rushing to get to school and to work. It's not a calm time in people's lives. We stay away from broadcasting in the morning. Similarly, the evening is a time people want to escape from the day's work. They don't want to see a nonprofit then. There's too much escapism programming to compete with.

The right time is daytime.

What Are DRTV Donors Like?

TV donors are generally younger than donors with other mediums. Amnesty International and World Wildlife Fund have DRTV donors who are well educated (but not as well educated as direct-mail donors) and younger than their typical direct-mail donors.

I like to think of my typical DRTV donor as a 35- to 45-year-old mother of two. The variation of that theme would be the DRTV donor for child sponsorship. Many of their DRTV donors are aged 60 and older.

Will DRTV Change?

I believe it won't change that much because a good story is a good story and a good offer is a good offer. Those things are timeless.

But it will change stylistically and technically. The techniques, packages, and graphics change. When I look back on our shows from TV years ago, they look dated. If we ran that show now, viewers could tell the show was made back then. It would bomb. The funny thing is, the stories are the same. They're about people's stories and making a difference in people's lives. Those things don't change in a decade.

The stories are now a bit shorter than they were 10 years ago, and I think that's a function of TV viewer attention spans being shorter.

If I had to make a list of the biggest trends in DRTV, they'd be:

• *Continued audience fragmentation.* This will put increasing pressure on nonprofit media budgets because fragmentation will mean a nonprofit will have to be in more places, with less viewers in each place, to find the same number of donors. It may mean nonprofits will fight harder with TV stations on broadcast fees.

• *Introduction of Web TV.* There are two boxes in people's houses—the computer and the TV. These two boxes will eventually be merged together for the general viewer. When that happens we need to understand the new DRTV dymamics of a two-way communication vehicle.

I think it's important to note that the leisure activity that's most impacted by the Internet is the computer. The place citizens decide to spend less time to spend more on the Net is the TV. We have to understand this medium, the Net, if we're to make effective use of their eventual convergence. And there's another important note: Studies have shown that people are more willing to use their credit card on-line than through the phone. Now, that's intriguing!

If we can link the TV's emotional storytelling with people's comfort with credit card use on-line, then convergence DRTV may be the most powerful fund-raising medium ever devised.

Incrementalism or a Revolution?

Why Direct-Mail Practitioners Can't Forget That the More Things Change, the More They Stay the Same

FRAN JACOBOWITZ AND KAY P. LAUTMAN

Someday the Internet and other new technologies may alter the way we practice direct-response fund-raising. But it won't eliminate direct-mail fund-raising tools. It may change the strategies, tactics, and production of direct-mail packages and programs, but direct mail is here to stay. So we still need to understand the immediate trends for this most important segment of direct-response fund-raising.

Twenty years ago, when personal computers first began appearing, the soothsayers were forecasting the end of the age of the printed word. They prophesized that books and magazines would disappear, and we would all be reading "on-screen." But it didn't happen. In fact, more books are registered each year in the Library of Congress than the previous year. In 1995, 359,437 titles were added. Clearly, there will always be books. However, what we mean by the term "book" is expanding to include electronic publishing, which means that the shape of the book will never be the same.

Similarly, direct-mail fund-raising hasn't disappeared since the addition of computerized communication systems. Rather, the opposite has taken place: The volume of nonprofit direct-mail packages sent in the United States and in other Western countries has increased over the last two decades. It seems that people still like to feel, touch, read, and respond to direct mail, and probably always will. But what we mean by direct mail may change over time to include other forms of electronic publishing.

A comparable prognostication emerged with the advent of telemarketing. When telemarketers first began calling in the early 1980s, there was some concern that it would drive direct mail out of business. Today we know that the most effective and efficient use of the phone for fund-raising turns out to be in conjunction with direct mail, not instead of it. That's because a synergy is created when multiple channels of communication are offered to donors.

Now it's the turn of Internet marketers to discover the potent synergy among direct-response media. In fact, we're starting to see direct mail used to drive traffic to Web sites. Postcards touting the advantages of various sites are now appearing in mailboxes. Direct mail appeals direct us to the Web site, asking us to make "instantaneous" gifts.

However, it's important to know that even when they get to the Web site, most people aren't making donations. In fact, according to the 1999 Melman Group Study of on-line activism, conducted for Craver, Mathews, Smith and Company, only about 8 percent of those who have Internet access say they are willing to make a donation to a charity or public interest group on-line. Granted, those with Internet access constitute a huge market—about 125 million citizens in the United States have access to the Internet every day. But it's not everyone. Most important, these are not Internet *donors;* they are people who "said" they would give on the Web.

On-line fund-raising is not for every cause. International relief and organizations like the Red Cross clearly do well on the Web when crises strike and activist causes like the ACLU are starting to turn the Web into an effective fund-raising tool. But the jury is still out for the majority of non-profit organizations. In the final analysis, just as in direct mail, some organizations will do well on the Web and some won't. It's a matter of testing.

The right offer sent to the right person at the right time will always be more effective than the right offer sent to the wrong person—or even the right offer sent at the wrong time. And since we as fund-raisers can't know what the right time is for any individual donor (even with more sophisticated databases), we have to keep giving them multiple opportunities to respond to our messages. Internet opportunities, telemarketing opportunities, and direct-mail opportunities.

Indeed, while major new tools appear to be available to direct-mail fund-raisers, it is critical to remember that most are the result of incremental changes that have improved the bottom line only slightly. The underlying concepts and principles of direct-mail fund-raising remain the same. New technologies are not going to create a revolution in direct-mail fund-raising, they are simply going to give us chances to do more testing to move the field incrementally to better profitability and effectiveness.

When the older of the two authors of this chapter (we won't say which) first started working in direct-mail fund-raising, a standard acquisition package consisted of the following:

- A one-page letter on letterhead that listed the board of directors, usually signed by a celebrity in the field.

- A two-color brochure with photographs, giving additional information on the organization.
- A wallet-flap postage paid reply envelope on which the donor/member wrote his or her own name and address. The envelope was precoded to indicate list source.
- Sometimes another enclosure, such as a newspaper reprint featuring the organization or a shorter endorsement note, was included.

Inevitably, the above contents were mailed in a closed-face, #10 envelope, with a first-class stamp. The #10 envelopes were hand-typed by "home workers" who took home boxes and boxes of 3 × 5-inch index cards with the names, addresses and giving histories of donors. They then typed or hand-wrote the address on each envelope. (Those boxes of file cards, by the way, were the database.) That's how it was done in the days before computerization. Segmentation consisted of "up to $20," "$20–$99.99," and "$100 and over." Multidonors were easy to identify. They were the people with several index cards stapled together.

Does any of this sound familiar today—some 35 years later?

Probably not as a whole; perhaps in part. Today it's more likely that the acquisition letter is four pages, directors are not listed, and the signer is the director of the organization, not a celebrity. Brochures (except for museums and other instances where four color seems appropriate) usually depress response rates. Reply envelopes are simply envelopes, sometimes postage-paid and sometimes not, depending on the organization. Instead of the donor having to write his or her name on the envelope used to return the check, the donor receives a precoded response form personalized with his or her name and address. This address shows through a window carrier envelope (not always a #10 and rarely closed-face), and certainly postage on acquisition mail is at the nonprofit rate, whether by stamp, meter, or indicia.

So how did we get from a one-page letter with a brochure to a four-page letter without? Or from a closed-face, first-class envelope to a window envelope with third-class postage, while maintaining similar rates of return and cost/benefit ratios?

In the early days, we "thought" that people wouldn't read a letter longer than one page (and that if they wanted more information they would read the brochure) . . . that window envelopes (because they contained only bills and advertisements) would automatically be trashed . . . and so on.

As we now know we were wrong in many cases. But were we wrong *then*—or did yesteryear's techniques simply become outmoded? Did third-class postage become more cost-effective because of the volume of mail generated by the growing competition—or would it have worked all along?

Surely hand-typed envelopes pull better, or we wouldn't insist on closed-faced, first-class envelopes to our high-dollar donors. And doesn't a longer letter always work better than an old-fashioned short letter that doesn't explain much? If this is true, why do so many organizations, such as the Red Cross and numerous health and veterans organizations, use short letters?

One simple answer is that closed-faced envelopes with lasered addresses (indistinguishable from hand-typed addresses, and just about the only way to "hand-type" a mass-produced letter in today's technologically driven world)—or even hand-addressed envelopes—usually garner a better response rate. The unfortunate fact is that the cost to use these techniques is so high that organizations reserve this use for their donor file mailings, where the return is usually at least five times higher than the return on acquisition mailings. In addition, for some organizations, the only way to make the technique cost effective is to reserve this special treatment for higher dollar donors ($50 or $100+).

The answer to the often-asked question of long letter versus short letter is that, no, longer letters don't always work better. In fact, some of the early tenets of direct mail are still valid, despite the fact that the format and components of the typical new package have changed. This is because what works for organizations that are literally household words (such as the Salvation Army, Easter Seals, and the March of Dimes) is different from (and shorter than) what is necessary for an organization with little name recognition. In the latter case, more explanation, indeed more salesmanship, is required.[1]

And just how did we gain all this newfound wisdom?

We stopped relying on what we personally believed to be true and started testing. Through "scientific," quantifiable testing, we learned that, no matter how counterintuitive, facts are facts. For example:

- Envelope teaser copy and photos often depress returns, especially on house file mailings.

---

[1]The use of new technologies such as the Internet may begin to challenge some of our tenets on long versus short letters because a short letter might offer a Web site address where a supporter could go to continue a story and solicitation. But like any good direct-mail fundraising endeavor, this letter/Web synergy would need to be tested very carefully.

- New acquisition packages (assumedly better) rarely beat the control.
- Inclusion of photographs (except those of animals) will lower response for many organizations.
- Donors have very different hot buttons. Some people respond only to premiums, some to emergencies, and others to virtually anything. Understanding your donor's preferred giving habits can save a great deal of money.

All of these truisms were developed through the step-by-step process of testing. The cardinal rule of testing is to test one thing at a time. You cannot test two variables simultaneously, no matter how minor. For example, you can't send one-half of your mailing with a response device directing donors to the Web site and eliminate the Web address from the other half, if you plan to include a brochure on the Web site in the first half. If you do, you will never know whether it was the response device alone that increased or depressed returns or the addition of the brochure.

Further, you must mail quantifiable numbers in order to get valid results. This means that you must mail a sufficient amount to get 100 returns on any one segment. For example, if you mail a 20,000-piece house file divided into two test panels (with every other name going into each segment) and get a 10 percent return, you will have 1,000 returns in each segment—10 times the amount necessary for a statistically valid test. In theory, this file could support testing more than one item.

If you have only a 4,000-piece mailing on which you expect only a 5 percent return, you can still test because each half of the test will consist of 2,000 pieces. If returns come in as expected at 5 percent each segment would have 100 returns.

You get the idea. The fewer names you have, the fewer things you can verify on tests.

But *what* should you test? Well, the envelope is a *part* of the package. So is the ask amount, postage rate, type face, enclosure or brochure, Business Return Envelope or Carrier Return Envelope, reply form, copy, art, letter signer, benefits package, and so on. Each of these elements is considered a "thing" in testing. You can test only one "thing" at a time, unless you have a large file that can be segmented—or if you want to test an entirely new package against an existing one.

If you want to test two new things in a mailing (and there are often valid reasons for testing more than one thing), you must create three mail panels or test lists and test your control (original) package against each of your new items. You should not split a mailing of 20,000 three ways if you anticipate your response rate to be just 1 percent—just because you want to test two different things. You'll need to be patient and save a test for next time, because splitting three ways would give panels of 6,660 pieces each. At a 1 percent response rate, each panel would only garner 67 responses—not enough to rely on the results of the test. Remember, each panel must be large enough to provide at least 100 responses.

In deciding what to test, it's very important to set a goal. Whatever the test is, is should be designed to do one of the following:

- Increase the average gift
- Increase the response rate
- Reduce the cost of the mailing

If it isn't expected to do one of these three things, it really isn't worth testing, particularly since testing will almost always, in the short run, add to the cost of the mailing. Of course, if the winner is less expensive overall, it's worth it.

Here are six general guidelines and rules for testing:

1. In general, test only one thing at a time—unless you have experience with testing or a file large enough to support multiple test panels.
2. Mail test packages within the same week. Conditions in the world change rapidly. A devastating hurricane in Florida that occurs between mailings produces vastly different market conditions for each package. The results will reflect such differences.
3. Mail test packages at the same postal rate, unless it is postage you are testing.
4. Mail test packages to the same lists (or segments of your house file) and split the lists on an nth (random sample) selection. In other words, a test in which half the mailing goes to one zip code and half goes to another is not a valid test. Splitting the file A–M and N–Z is not random either.
5. Test in sufficient quantities for valid results.
6. After test results are in, test the same thing once again to validate your findings.

It's important to remember that things change. What worked two, three, or four years ago needs to be retested today.

Envelope Teasers

A perfect example of this is a campaign that Lautman & Company created to raise funds to build the Smithsonian Institution's National Museum of the American Indian. When the campaign was introduced in 1991, a "Mask" envelope package was introduced as the control. Because best practices in direct marketing, regardless of medium, demand testing, the envelope was tested against this very plain envelope that simply said "Your Charter Invitation Enclosed."

At first, the results for this test seemed contradictory. The "Charter Invitation" package (see Exhibit 6.1) had a lower cost to raise a dollar (CTRAD), and an average gift nearly $1 higher than the control. But the "Mask" (see Exhibit 6.2) had a response rate that was nearly 10 percent higher—bringing in significantly more donors. This is where a clear definition of the goals of a particular project helps. In this instance, the goal of

---

EXHIBIT 6.1   Smithsonian NMAI Plain Envelope

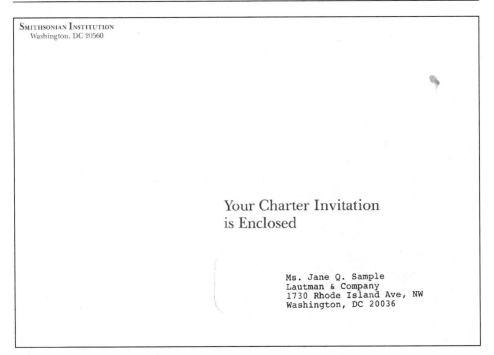

SMITHSONIAN INSTITUTION
Washington, DC 20560

Your Charter Invitation
is Enclosed

Ms. Jane Q. Sample
Lautman & Company
1730 Rhode Island Ave, NW
Washington, DC 20036

Used with permission from NMAI.

the mailing is to acquire new donors. Which package does a better job of acquiring new donors? The "Mask."

By extrapolating these results, we can look at the case for the "Mask" envelope in a different light. If the size of the mailing were 500,000 pieces, instead of a small test panel, the Mask envelope would bring in 5,800 new donors. The "charter invitation" envelope would bring in just 5,300 new donors. If, over the next year, 10 percent of the additional 500 donors gave a second gift equal to the amount of the acquisition gift, additional money would be earned. This 10 percent response rate is a conservative number but still represents significantly more money than the additional cost to use the Mask package.

Throughout the campaign, we continued envelope testing, leaving all other elements of the package identical. The next "winner" was a variation on the Mask envelope, which not only increased response rates (goal #1) but also appreciably reduced the cost of the package (goal #2), because we eliminated the cost of four-color printing. (See Exhibit 6.3.)

EXHIBIT 6.2   **Smithsonian NMAI Mask Envelope**

Used with permission from NMAI.

Here there was no question which was the winning package. The "teaser-only" package had a higher response rate and an equivalent average gift. But as the package continued to mail, we continued to test. During the mid-1990s, this package became a winner. Again, the results were clear-cut: a 26 percent increase in response rate for the text envelope and a cost to raise a dollar that was $0.03 lower.

Even though the "text" envelope had a higher cost per thousand to produce because of the graphics, the large increase in response rate justified making it the new control. Not surprisingly, there were other envelopes in the mail for other causes and products at the time that used this same graphic heavy approach. We were riding a trend.

This envelope was the winner for quite a long time. But times change, and new trends appear. After several tests, including envelopes, message, and brochure, this entirely different package became the control. The package offers a small gift—a pressure-sensitive label with the potential donor's name and address (a "name sticker"). (See Exhibit 6.4.)

EXHIBIT 6.3   Smithsonian NMAI Text Envelope

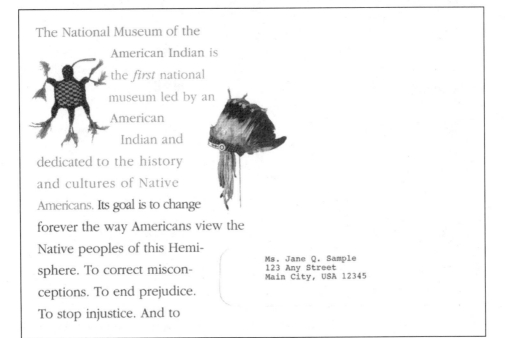

The National Museum of the American Indian is the *first* national museum led by an American Indian and dedicated to the history and cultures of Native Americans. Its goal is to change forever the way Americans view the Native peoples of this Hemisphere. To correct misconceptions. To end prejudice. To stop injustice. And to

Ms. Jane Q. Sample
123 Any Street
Main City, USA 12345

Used with permission from NMAI.

EXHIBIT 6.4   Smithsonian NMAI Name Sticker Package Graphic

Jane Sample
Lautman & Company
1730 Rhode Island Avenue, NW
Suite 700
Washington, DC 20036

Jane Sample
Lautman & Company
1730 Rhode Island Avenue, NW
Suite 700
Washington, DC 20036

Jane Sample
Lautman & Company
1730 Rhode Island Avenue, NW
Suite 700
Washington, DC 20036

Jane Sample
Lautman & Company
1730 Rhode Island Avenue, NW
Suite 700
Washington, DC 20036

Jane Sample
Lautman & Company
1730 Rhode Island Avenue, NW
Suite 700
Washington, DC 20036

Jane Sample
Lautman & Company
1730 Rhode Island Avenue, NW
Suite 700
Washington, DC 20036

Jane Sample
Lautman & Company
1730 Rhode Island Avenue, NW
Suite 700
Washington, DC 20036

Jane Sample
Lautman & Company
1730 Rhode Island Avenue, NW
Suite 700
Washington, DC 20036

Jane Sample
Lautman & Company
1730 Rhode Island Avenue, NW
Suite 700
Washington, DC 20036

Jane Sample
Lautman & Company
1730 Rhode Island Avenue, NW
Suite 700
Washington, DC 20036

Jane Sample
Lautman & Company
1730 Rhode Island Avenue, NW
Suite 700
Washington, DC 20036

Jane Sample
Lautman & Company
1730 Rhode Island Avenue, NW
Suite 700
Washington, DC 20036

REMEMBER
the Past...

IMAGINE
the Future.

REMEMBER
the Past...
IMAGINE
the Future.

REMEMBER
the Past...
IMAGINE
the Future.

REMEMBER
the Past...

IMAGINE
the Future.

REMEMBER
the Past...

IMAGINE
the Future.

REMEMBER
the Past...
IMAGINE
the Future.

REMEMBER
the Past...
IMAGINE
the Future.

REMEMBER
the Past...

IMAGINE
the Future.

Jane Sample
Lautman & Company
1730 Rhode Island Avenue, NW
Suite 700
Washington, DC 20036

Jane Sample
Lautman & Company
1730 Rhode Island Avenue, NW
Suite 700
Washington, DC 20036

Jane Sample
Lautman & Company
1730 Rhode Island Avenue, NW
Suite 700
Washington, DC 20036

Jane Sample
Lautman & Company
1730 Rhode Island Avenue, NW
Suite 700
Washington, DC 20036

Jane Sample
Lautman & Company
1730 Rhode Island Avenue, NW
Suite 700
Washington, DC 20036

Jane Sample
Lautman & Company
1730 Rhode Island Avenue, NW
Suite 700
Washington, DC 20036

Jane Sample
Lautman & Company
1730 Rhode Island Avenue, NW
Suite 700
Washington, DC 20036

Jane Sample
Lautman & Company
1730 Rhode Island Avenue, NW
Suite 700
Washington, DC 20036

Jane Sample
Lautman & Company
1730 Rhode Island Avenue, NW
Suite 700
Washington, DC 20036

Jane Sample
Lautman & Company
1730 Rhode Island Avenue, NW
Suite 700
Washington, DC 20036

Used with permission from NMAI.

EXHIBIT 6.4   Continued

Your personalized mailing labels
         are enclosed—and they look great!

Jane Sample
Lautman & Company
1730 Rhode Island Avenue, NW
Suite 700
Washington, DC 20036

|.|.|||..||.....||.||.|.|.|

Name and Address Label Packages

Many major nonprofits—including environmental groups like the National Wildlife Federation and the Wilderness Society, cultural organizations like the Kennedy Center and Colonial Williamsburg Foundation, health organizations like Memorial Sloan Kettering Cancer Center, and civil rights groups like the Southern Poverty Law Center—have used name and address labels on a widespread basis. While name stickers have been around for a very long time, up until the late 1990s many organizations shunned their use because of the public's "knee-jerk" response to packages like these, which means a high response rate and low average gift.

To counter this truism about name sticker packages, many organizations have developed an acquisition strategy that includes more than one control package. In this strategy, one track focuses on name stickers, while an additional track uses a more traditional direct-mail approach, relying on a well-constructed case for giving and an "ask" appealing to the donor's philanthropic nature. Donors acquired from a more traditional appeal renew better, although they are more costly to acquire. The underlying trend here, however, is to offset the high cost of acquiring "high-quality" donors using the subsidy provided by the "lower"-quality name sticker donors. Will this strategy work in the long run? Only careful analysis for each organization, including sophisticated backend and lifetime value analysis, will tell.

Although name stickers were appropriate for this particular organization at this particular time, you can't assume they are necessarily right for you. If you want to try something the competition is doing, first try to figure out what it is about the "look" that makes it work and then test carefully.

Types of Name Stickers

Name sticker packages for both acquisition and house appeals have experienced change over the years. In the late 1980s, the style of name sticker was very different. They were usually two-color labels, gummed together at one edge, similar to a very small notepad. They had to be moistened to be affixed to an envelope—and often the glue wasn't very good.

The first major shift in name stickers was toward pressure-sensitive labels. If you look in your mailbox today, you can see that these labels are clearly favored over the old-fashioned glue-back ones. In fact, there is now only one supplier in the United States that can manufacture the "old-fashioned" kind. But who knows? Ten years from now, the "old-fashioned" kind could come back into favor. Nothing is static—so testing needs to take place all the time. It's one of the things that never changes. Over the last ten years, moving over to pressure-sensitive was just one of the changes for name stickers. Today many labels are four-color or embossed with gold or silver foil. The theory behind this change is that a four-color label has a higher perceived value and therefore is more likely to elicit a donation.

But is this valid theory? Well, Lautman & Company tested the theory over a two-year period for the AARP Andrus Foundation, a 501(c) 3 organization dedicated to research on aging.

The initial acquisition test was a two-color label (blue and black) featuring an inkwell/feather pen (see Exhibit 6.5) against a four-color label. This symbol was chosen because the foundation's logo uses a stylized feather and, coincidentally, the executive director's name was Dr. John Feather. The other package depicted "puppies and kitties." This art was chosen arbitrarily after consultation with colleagues at other agencies who were mailing millions of name sticker packages per year. (See Exhibit 6.6.)

The winner? Puppies and kitties, hands down, especially in percent return, which is what acquisition is all about. But we continued to test the images—and these more colorful images are the current control. (See Exhibit 6.7.) We'll continue testing, however, because tastes change, and trends evolve.

EXHIBIT 6.5   AARP Name Stickers—Feather and Inkwell Package

Jane Sample 1730 Rhode Island Ave Washington DC 20036	Jane Sample 1730 Rhode Island Ave Washington DC 20036	Jane Sample 1730 Rhode Island Ave Washington DC 20036
Jane Sample 1730 Rhode Island Ave Washington DC 20036	Jane Sample 1730 Rhode Island Ave Washington DC 20036	Jane Sample 1730 Rhode Island Ave Washington DC 20036
Jane Sample 1730 Rhode Island Ave Washington DC 20036	Jane Sample 1730 Rhode Island Ave Washington DC 20036	Jane Sample 1730 Rhode Island Ave Washington DC 20036
Jane Sample 1730 Rhode Island Ave Washington DC 20036	Jane Sample 1730 Rhode Island Ave Washington DC 20036	Jane Sample 1730 Rhode Island Ave Washington DC 20036
Jane Sample 1730 Rhode Island Ave Washington DC 20036	Jane Sample 1730 Rhode Island Ave Washington DC 20036	Jane Sample 1730 Rhode Island Ave Washington DC 20036
Jane Sample 1730 Rhode Island Ave Washington DC 20036	Jane Sample 1730 Rhode Island Ave Washington DC 20036	Jane Sample 1730 Rhode Island Ave Washington DC 20036

Used with permission from AARP. Copyright AARP Andrus Foundation, 1998.

Use of Colorful Premiums

In fact, the use of more and stronger colors may be a trend in acquisition. We've seen success in improving acquisition for various organizations when using a four-color "tipped-on" membership card. This is a plasticized card that is spot-glued onto the reply device and shows through a second window in the reply envelope. The graphics are eye-catching, and

EXHIBIT 6.6   AARP Name Stickers—Puppies and Kitties Package

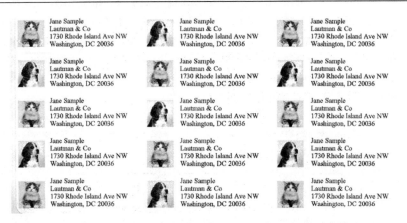

Used with permission from AARP. Copyright AARP Andrus Foundation, 1999.

EXHIBIT 6.7   AARP Name Stickers—Sun and Moon Package

Used with permission from AARP. Copyright AARP Andrus Foundation, 1999.

the perceived value of this type of card is higher than a paper card or two-color one. In one case, this innovation helped beat a control that had been in place for five years.

Premiums can be used, and tested, in house appeals too. Most common are calendar and/or card programs, like those produced for the National Museum of the American Indian, the United States Holocaust Memorial Museum, the National Museum of Women in the Arts, GMHC (Gay Men's Health Crisis), the Central Park Conservancy, and others. (See Exhibit 6.8.)

The reason notecards and wall calendars are chosen most often as the premium is because despite their relatively low cost to produce, they have a strong perceived value—usually close to most organization's average gift size. In addition, cards and calendars are disposable, items you will need more of in the future.

In selecting art, it is important to remember three things:

1. Photographs have proven through testing to work better for calendars; artwork tests better for cards.
2. Choose calendar photos of scenes people will want to look at day in and day out.
3. Choose "popular" art for the cards, shying away from your own good taste.

EXHIBIT 6.8   Gay Men's Health Crisis 1997 Spring Card Package

Used with permission from Gay Men's Health Crisis.

Each of these premium programs works similarly.

An announcement letter is sent to the donor, advising him or her that a free gift (specified and described) will be arriving shortly in the mail. This package includes a letter describing the premium and restating the case for support. The letter also clearly states that there is no obligation on the part of the donor and offers the opportunity to "opt out" of receiving the gift. Typical response rates on announcement letters range from 5 to 8 percent, with average gifts from $15 to $50, depending on the cause.

Six to eight weeks later, the premium itself follows. Here response rates increase, sometimes to as high as 12 to 15 percent, depending, as always, on the organization and the perceived value of the premium itself. Finally, another six to eight weeks later, the third part of the program, the follow-up, is sent. This simple package, usually monarch size, confirms that the donor received the gift, reiterates that there is no obligation, and gives the donor another chance to make a contribution. Response rates here are similar to that of the announcement package or slightly lower.

As you can imagine, a complete series like this has innumerable areas available for testing. Right now, teasers of the instructional type "I've reserved a special gift in your name," "Your 1999 Members' Only Calendar Enclosed," and "Did you receive the gift I sent you?" are still holding their own. However, the no-teaser trend appears to be creeping into this area of mail too. Ask string tests, postage tests—whatever you want to try to use to increase the average gift, cut the cost, or obtain more gifts—are fair game for testing. Who knows what the look of premium programs will metamorphose into as testing continues?

Plain Carrier Envelopes

Recent envelope testing reveals a trend toward using fewer graphics. Plain envelopes are winning most tests, particularly for house file mailings. Why? Perhaps because the packages with heavy graphics look too commercial and the plainer envelope looks like a "real" letter. It's not too surprising, in the days of e-mail and high-tech everything, that more personal direct mail is working, because people are still people, after all, and the human touch still matters.

For example, in this capital campaign mail appeal for the Japanese American National Museum, everyone agreed that the graphics were beautiful. (See Exhibit 6.9.) However, just because we all liked it doesn't mean it was the winner. In fact, the simpler envelope generated slightly more responses, a higher average gift, and a lower cost to raise a dollar. (See Exhibit 6.10.)

Although the number of additional gifts wasn't dramatic, running the numbers out show that the plain envelope won significantly. By multiplying the additional number of gifts by the high average gift, we learned that the plain envelope brought in significantly more income than the graphic one. Coupled with the fact that, in the future, printing plain envelopes will cost less than graphically rich ones, the margin grows even larger. One could argue that this is a special instance, because it is a capital campaign, or because the museum has a unique audience—those who care about the history and experiences of Japanese Americans in the United States. However, we are finding the same results holding true for many other organizations. Tests were conducted for house appeals for the Coalition for the Homeless, Central Park Conservancy, and the National Museum of Women in the Arts, among others. In all instances, the plain carrier won, and some won quite convincingly.

EXHIBIT 6.9   Japanese American National Museum—November 1998 Acquisition Pavilion Test with Graphic

JAPANESE AMERICAN
NATIONAL MUSEUM
369 East First Street
Los Angeles, California 90012

PLEASE
JOIN US...

A1BC
Jane Sample
Lautman & Company
1730 Rhode Island Ave.
Suite 700
Washington, DC   20036

Used with permission from Japanese American National Museum.

EXHIBIT 6.10   Japanese American National Museum—November 1998 Acquisition Pavilion Test, Plain Package

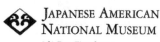

JAPANESE AMERICAN
NATIONAL MUSEUM
369 East First Street
Los Angeles, California 90012

RSVP

Jane Q. Sample
Lautman & Co.
1730 Rhode Island Ave NW
Suite 700
Washington, DC 20036

Used with permission from Japanese American National Museum.

This was certainly true when we tested this for the Coalition for the Homeless. In this case, not only was the response rate significantly higher, but the average gift was as well. Discovering where an organization fits into package trends can mean significantly more money on the bottom line.

The trend toward simpler packages is beginning to show up in acquisitions as well. Tests for the House of Ruth, a local women's shelter in the Washington, D.C., area, as well as Ronald McDonald House of New York show the plain envelope outpulling the graphic and/or teaser envelope, sometimes significantly. (See Exhibit 6.11A and B.) A word of caution. Both of

---

EXHIBIT 6.11A   Ronald McDonald House—Acquisition Package with No Teaser Copy

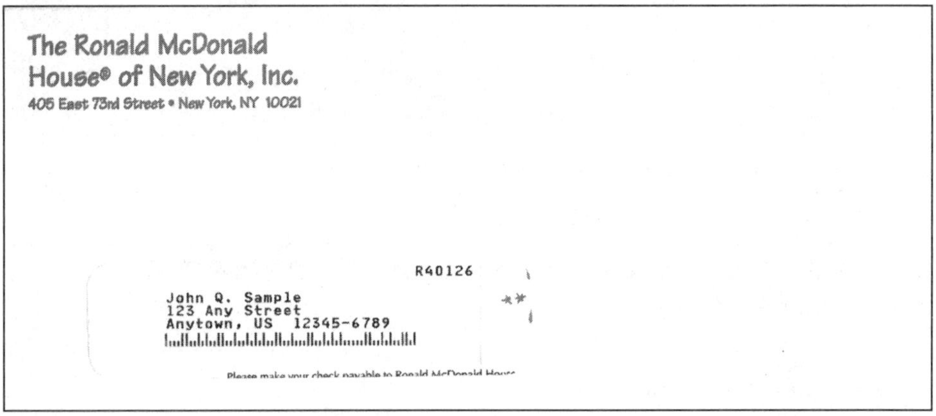

The Ronald McDonald
House® of New York, Inc.
405 East 73rd Street • New York, NY 10021

R40126

John Q. Sample
123 Any Street
Anytown, US   12345-6789

Please make your check payable to Ronald McDonald House

Used with permission from Ronald McDonald House.

EXHIBIT 6.11B   Ronald McDonald House—Acquisition Package with Teaser Copy

"The House That Love Built"

Jane Q. Sample
Lautman & Co
1730 Rhode Island Ave
Washington, DC 20036

Used with permission from Ronald McDonald House.

these organizations have high name recognition, Ronald McDonald House nationally and House of Ruth locally. This may be a factor of this test—yet another reason why each organization must test each trend for itself.

In this instance, the "no teaser" envelope lifted response dramatically. Clearly, this is an area that warrants testing for almost all organizations, because the effect on the bottom line can be significant.

But the trend toward simple carrier envelopes doesn't hold true for every organization. In fact, for the Central Park Conservancy, a New York–based group dedicated to supporting and maintaining Central Park, the opposite proved true. (See Exhibit 6.12.) However, because this is counter to the prevailing trend, and because the results were not particularly dramatic in terms of response rate, further testing is clearly warranted. Remember that one test is not sufficient. You must confirm all tests with a second test.

For Central Park, response rates were virtually the same, but the average gift on the teaser envelope was higher by $10. This could be a one-time occurrence—or a trend—or a real difference in the way that donors on this file perform. One test isn't enough to establish valid parameters for making sweeping changes. What if you're reading the results of the test wrong? Or what if it's just an anomaly? A lot of money could be at risk. That's why testing more than once is imperative.

Challenging the status quo is also extremely important in direct-mail testing. For years the prepaid business reply envelope (BRE) was the standard. Recent testing indicates a trend in house file mailings away from BREs toward envelopes with no postage at all (courtesy reply envelope—CRE) or envelopes with an actual first-class stamp on it. If successful, using a CRE can save a lot of money. Using a first-class stamp on an envelope can be expensive, but those who are successfully using them report significantly higher response rates and higher average gifts. But these trends are not rules of thumb. Responses to these tests differ by organization. Donors to some groups still show a preference for the BRE. Others do better with a CRE. One preciously held idea is that you can save dollars by including the phrase "Your stamp here helps us save much-needed funds." Results of several tests (counterintuitive, but accurate) show that this message actually can depress both percent response and average gift.

We urge testing of this phase for all organizations. This is a cutting-edge area—and one that challenges our notion of "what always works." It's the perfect example of why testing needs to be done continuously: because the market changes. While the results for an organization may be

---

EXHIBIT 6.12   Central Park Conservancy—April 1999 Card Program

---

Used with permission from Central Park Conservancy.

different, it is clear that assumptions are dangerous and that even a tiny change can make a major difference.

Personalized Packages

Some areas of package development are more affected by trends than others. For the most part (and there are always exceptions), fully personalized packages perform better for high-dollar donors, usually defined as donors with a most recent contribution (MRC) of $100 or more. But if the quantity to be mailed is large enough to warrant, test for yourself. Every file responds differently.

For those of you who assume that all donors need a fully personalized package, test a less expensive "Dear Friend" letter to those donors whose highest previous contribution (HPC) was less than $100. When the House of Ruth tested this for the first time, the results were surprising, because personalization of the higher dollar segments actually depressed results.

Don't rely on your instincts in direct mail—or in any other direct-response medium. You could be wrong, even though it doesn't make sense.

Testing Typefaces on Letters

In general, some areas of testing have more effect than others. One area for testing is typeface. Before the advent of computers, there were two main typewriter typefaces, pica and elite. When IBM Selectric typewriters became the office standard, the typeface of choice became Courier—mostly because everyone had it. It didn't hurt that it was an eminently readable typeface. In the early 1990s—before every laser printer offered hundreds of typefaces—Courier remained the standard. But with the advent of third- and fourth-generation word processing programs came Times Roman as a new standard for letters. The question for direct mail practitioners became: "Does it matter what typeface we use?"

In the beginning, many moved over to Times Roman without testing. Others stayed with Courier, because it looked like the letter was written on a typewriter and thus was theoretically more personal. What did it matter? It was just a typeface.

In direct mail, even the smallest detail (and sometimes the seemingly most innocuous) can have a profound effect on response rates. And testing for typefaces has shown that, like almost everything else discussed here, the answer depends on the particular organization. For some, particularly those with older donors, Courier works better. For others, Times Roman is the winner. And for the fortunate few, it doesn't really affect response rate. So once again, the most important way to know what a particular trend means to any one organization is to test that trend.

Do Credit Card Offers Work?

The same is true for credit cards. In the beginning (way back in 1990), when many organizations began to have the ability to process credit cards, the option began to appear on response devices. However, as time went on, direct mailers began to challenge the assumption that offering the credit card option was innocuous. For some it is, having virtually no effect on response rates or average gifts. For others, it depresses response rate. (Surprise!) For the lucky few, it increases both the average gift and the response rate. The lesson here: Leave no element untested.

Web Sites and E-Mail Addresses

One of today's trends is to make sure that every piece of stationery, including the letterhead and reply device, includes the Web site and e-mail address. Sounds good—and couldn't possibly hurt, could it? Well, could it? We don't know, because we haven't yet initiated those tests. But you can rest assured they will be done, because no one really knows the answer: Does it helps or hurt?

Those with Web sites that can accept donations via credit card are actively encouraging the capture of e-mail addresses on direct-mail response devices. The theory behind this new trend is that some portion of those who give their e-mail address may be willing to renew electronically. The assumption is that electronic renewals will be less costly than direct mail renewals. Some even venture to say that electronic renewals will have better response rates. All of this may be true, but the caveat is: test, test, test. Asking for an e-mail address may hurt response rate in the mail—and may not increase electronic renewals. This entire area of inter-activity with the Web requires tests that are carefully designed to measure not only the direct-mail side of the response but also the electronic side. What good is an e-mail address if it depresses direct-mail response and doesn't provide a corresponding lift in Web-based revenue generation? On the other hand, if the technique proves to reduce costs for renewals with no harm to the revenue side, then go for it. But please, test it first, because the goal is always to earn as much money as possible.

And please pay attention to new media! As the Internet quickly becomes a medium that reaches an affluent section of society every day, fund-raisers need to pay close attention to the impact synergistic strategies have on direct-response fund-raising. A good example of this comes from Greenpeace Argentina. In 1999 Greenpeace Argentina ran a successful direct-response television fund-raising program. The 15- and 30-minute "infomercials" explain the organization's work and ask prospective donors to pick up the phone to make a gift right away. Approximately 10 percent of the gifts that came through the TV show came from donors going to their computers and making an on-line gift. That is significant enough to make or break any fund-raising program. However, Greenpeace doesn't know whether on-line giving has reduced the phone gifts and reduced or increased the total dollars raised through the TV campaign.

Marcelo Iniarra Iraegui, fund-raising director of Greenpeace Argentina, is now beginning systematic testing of the impact of the Internet on his TV campaign. He'll test the effect of inserting a one-minute advertisement for on-line giving and also test the impact of listing the URL at the bottom of the screen—and for how long. More fund-raisers need to integrate this kind of rigor between new and old direct response media.

Upgrading Techniques

One way to earn more money is to try to upgrade the average gift of the existing donor. In most house appeals, the amount requested is personalized for each donor and is usually based on the amount of a previous gift. The question is—which gift? The most recent gift (MRC)? The highest previous gift (HPC)? This is a perfect opportunity to test. The goal here, maintaining or upgrading the gift, offers many testing opportunities. One that can provide unexpected results is testing a multiple ask string versus a single ask. This could be based on either MRC or HPC, and could include a multiple that looks like this:

[ ] 1X HPC   [ ] 1.5X HPC   [ ] 2X HPC $_____Other

In the above example, the ask string for a donor with a highest previous contribution of $50.00 would be as follows:

[ ]$50   [ ]$75   [ ]$100 $_____Other

This could test against a reply device with only the HPC and "other" as choices.

[ ]HPC $ Other_____

Testing often identifies the counterintuitive nature of direct marketing, as mentioned several times earlier. For example, for many years, it has been common practice to attempt to get donors to upgrade their gifts by circling the second ask in a gift string and urging the donor to upgrade to this amount using a handwritten request on the reply device. Recent results of testing show that this technique is *depressing* average gifts rather than increasing them. Why do we think this trend against suggested gifts is appearing? In the first place, we aren't entirely sure that it's actually a new trend. Perhaps we're just testing something that has always suppressed results. And if it is a trend, it may because of the increasing sophistication of the direct-mail donor.

Donors today are receiving mail at an astonishing rate. It would be naïve to think that our donors don't look at our techniques and figure out what's going on. It would be hard to believe that there's anyone out there today who doesn't know that computers are generating all those "personalized" letters. When we're all using the same techniques trying to improve performance, some donors are sure to catch on. Even if they don't articulate it, they know when they've had enough of any particular trend, idea, or technique. Donors communicate their displeasure, or boredom, or sense of overkill by not responding. So when response rates to a particular technique start to fall, that's when it's time to test against it, to look for something new, or to change strategies entirely. But when you do, be certain to test.

You Get What You Ask For

What is your basic offer in acquisition? Should you start at $15? $25 $30? This is one of the most difficult areas in all direct marketing itself. There is no simple answer—and no guiding trend.

But before the board of directors makes a sweeping directive to increase the price of membership, please make sure you test. This is one of the most sensitive areas in direct mail. We have conducted numerous tests for nonprofits and know that there is a threshold for each particular organization. Museums offering tangible benefits can ask for a larger gift than organizations offering no benefits at all. Organizations offering direct service to individuals often can tie the gift request to a specific need, such as "Your gift of $25 will feed a family of four for a week." Health charities and research institutions often find average gift under $15—sometimes as low as $10. Due to intense competition in the environmental arena, we have seen initial acquisition requests for gifts as low as $10. Local direct-service organizations with high name recognition can often ask for, and get, initial gifts in the $30 to $35 range. As you can see, the initial ask can be anywhere—so testing is imperative. Strange things happen with initial ask testing.

We were asked to help increase acquisition response rates for one client whose membership dues started at $50. We felt that this was a high initial gift for an organization that offers few tangible benefits and has a cause that is intellectual rather than emotional. Thus we tested a $35 entry level against the standard $50.

Although the cost to raise a dollar for each membership level was identical, the real breakthrough came in the response rate. Significantly more donations were made at the lower ask amount—and the cost to *acquire* each new member (total cost of the mailing/total number of new members) was $7.44 less for the $35 test panel. A subsequent test validated these results, and we are confident that donors at the new $35 level can be upgraded.

Can You Raise Your Dues?

Before increasing membership dues, you must test and calculate what change will mean to you. It's easy to assume that $5 more on a file of 25,000 will bring you at least $125,000—but look again. First of all, no one gets 100 percent renewal, and second, that $5 price hike will lose a number of donors for you. The relationship between loss and gain is critical. It's relatively easy, however, to test acquisition price increase. After all, your new donors weren't aware of the old (entry level) price or ask.

The Central Park Conservancy tested raising rather than lowering basic membership dues in acquisition from $35 to $40. The results show that when the dues were raised from $35 to $40, there was no immediate monetary loss because the increase in average gift at the higher level more than compensated for the lower response rate. This, however, is a shortsighted approach to acquisition and disregards the primary purpose of acquisition, which is to get new members. If, in the process, you happen to also make money, that's a wonderful side benefit. But it rarely happens. In the case of the Central Park Conservancy, it made the same amount of money, chiefly because of the very high average gift the acquisition package generates. (Most acquisition for this cause is sent to the zip codes surrounding Central Park, which include New York City's wealthiest addresses.)

What's really going on here is that the price increase suppresses the response rate and increases the average gift, which is exactly what asking for more money usually does. But the actual price for that higher average gift in this particular test was the loss of numerous potential members. Over time, there will be fewer members to renew—and therefore less money. That's why the conservancy didn't increase its dues. This concept is the basis for all sophisticated backend analysis: Is it better to get the money now or wait for the long haul? Sometimes the answer is: now. But everyone should be aware of the consequences of arbitrary decisions in direct mail, as opposed to relying on the incremental truth of testing.

The harder challenge is developing a meaningful test for renewals. Most membership renewals are based on a magazine-style series, with the program consisting of six or seven notices carefully timed around the member's annual expiration date. This means that every month, several different notices are being sent out. Unless your file has more than 200,000 donors, the size of each renewal notice group will likely be too small to give an accurate testing sample. Even if the file size is large enough to test, good practice requires that the test take place over time—going to at least three renewal groups, and preferably six months to a year's worth of renewals. When the results are finally compiled, interpreting them usually will require an extremely knowledgeable analyst, with access to the data in electronic media (Excel or another spreadsheet program). Only then can a fully calculated decision on the effects of increasing the basic dues be made. Most organizations don't have the luxury of such extensive testing. It's highly advisable, however, because the results can be—you guessed it—counterintuitive. Knowing what lies ahead can prevent a crisis down the road for the unprepared.

Changing Your Logo

Another area where organizations love to make change is in the area of logos. "Let's refresh our look," or "Let's change our name." This can spell disaster in direct mail. People open most envelopes because they recognize the sender—and the logo and/or look of the package is important to this recognition. If the change is inevitable—and sometimes it is—try to get permission to introduce the change gradually. Use the old logo on the outside of the envelope and the new logo on the letter and reply device for at least six months, if at all possible. Or put the name with the new logo for a transition period. Whatever you do, don't just change the logo. If you must just change it, test a panel of old logo versus new. At least when revenue is down, which will probably be the case, you will have known in advance what percentage fall-off to expect. You can always apologize to the board later for not following its instructions.

One organization for which we worked wanted to institute both a new logo and a dues increase. Because the organization was so well known to the public, the logo change, which it implemented without testing, was financially disastrous. After about six months, it returned to the familiar logo. When a $5-per-year dues increase was mandated ("Just the price of a hamburger and drink," said a board member), we were fortunate enough to argue successfully for a test. The results showed that both members and prospective members cared a great deal. The organization not only experienced a small actual loss from the dues increase side of the test, but projections showed that if the increase had been carried out, the ultimate net loss would have been enormous.

Conclusion

New technologies often demand revolutionary changes, whether they are appropriate to a sector or not. In direct-mail fund-raising, incremental change leads to more profitable direct-mail programs more often. And incrementalism finds its true expression in systematic testing that:

- Learns which trends in direct mail are changing.
- Uses the basic principles of direct mail to earn as much money as possible for each nonprofit organization.
- Learns what's working and what isn't.
- Sees how incremental changes in response rates can result in significant changes in the size of a membership file.
- Makes sure we don't implement large-scale assumptions without the benefit of information about the effects of the assumptions.

In this chapter, we've illustrated how a few things can change in direct mail. We've shown that it's important to test just about every element a direct-mail practitioner can imagine. But in the final analysis, most things have stayed the same. Letters still go in envelopes. Some things work for some organizations and don't work for others. In the final analysis—and until proven otherwise—direct mail remains one of the most cost-efficient ways for nonprofit organizations to ask for—and receive—support from the general public.

An Internet Direct Response Fund Raising Test Guide

The Internet and fund-raising are a very new partnership. In other areas of direct-response fund-raising, we have a long list of studies, books, practitioner results, and publications that provide a liturgy for direct-response fund-raising, especially direct mail. In deciding what to test online, it is very important to set a goal. Whatever the online test is, it should be designed to do one of the following:

- Simply acquire that first online gift
- Increase the online response rate
- Increase the online average gift

If it isn't expected to do one of these three things, it really isn't worth testing, particularly since testing will almost always, in the short run, add to the human resource and programming costs of on-line fund-raising. Of course, if the winning on-line fund-raising strategy is less expensive overall, it is worth it. It is also important to remember that many on-line fund-raising endeavors are loss leaders at the present, so any way organizations can reduce the ROI in on-line fund-raising (especially in prospecting for on-line donors), they should use testing to do just that.

Some general guidelines and rules for on-line fund-raising testing follow. Many of these may seem familiar. That's because the basic rules for testing on-line do not differ significantly from the basic rules for direct-mail testing. The more things change, the more they stay the same.

1. In general, test only one thing at a time—unless you have experience with testing, or a file large enough to support multiple test web pages. This is doubly important on-line because the ease of on-line publishing can lead to testitis!—too many tests at once. If you suc-cumb to the urge, you may actually invalidate all your results, and all your hard work will be for nought.

2. Launch test web areas or elements within the same day—or even hours. Conditions in the world change rapidly and things move even more rapidly on-line. The news that a devastating earthquake in Mexico City has just occurred may be read on-line almost immedi-ately by millions of users—and they might click immediately to a fund raising area. Even a one hour difference could ruin your test. Launch test areas and elements simultaneously.

3. House test areas and elements on servers that have the same capa-bilities. If one test page takes longer to download because it sits on a less capable computer, that could ruin a test. Studies from Sun Microsystems indicate that for every 10 seconds it takes for a Web page to download, you lose 10 percent of your visitors. Imagine how this could destroy an on-line test!

4. If you send out an e-mail solicitation, then send the e-solicitation to the same lists (or segments of your e-house file) and split the lists on an nth (random sample) selection. In other words, a test in which half

the mailing goes to addresses at aol.com and the other half goes to random ISP providers is not a valid test. Splitting the file A-M and N-Z is not random, either.

5. Conduct e-mail solicitation tests in sufficient quantities for valid results.
6. After test results are in, test the same thing once again to validate your findings.

Some testing ideas:

Because this is a new fund-raising medium, nonprofit organizations need to understand the basics of direct-response fund-raising on-line. Following on the idea that direct-mail fund-raising has much to teach us on-line, try to test the following:

Personalization. Nonprofit organizations are beginning to build personalization into their fund-raising Web sites. Visit an example at *www.alumni.utoronto.ca.* The University of Toronto allows an alumna to personalize her own alumni web page. Does this cookie-driven personalization improve the relationship with a supporter and improve fund-raising?

Conduct a test. Offer half of your on-line supporters the chance to personal-ize their experience with your organization's Web site. Do not give the other half the same personalized experience, but instead give them a more static experience. Now let them interact with your Web site and after a set period of time, send each group an e-mail solicitation and see which group gives more money to your organization.

Premiums. Upfront premiums in direct mail can improve lapsed renewal rates, acquisition response rates, and relationships with past supporters. On your Web site, test the efficacy of on-line premiums directly related to computers, such as screensavers, software, hardware, mousepads, a mouse, etc.

Calendar. In the introduction to this book, Mal Warwick mentioned that the annual cycle is an ecological human constant that shouldn't be ignored in any fund-raising endeavor—no matter the technology. This needs to be tested in the on-line environment. An e-mail solicitation cycle should be created that follows the traditional times of the year for solicitation (whether it is a special appeal, annual renewal, or reminder); this cycle should be tested against a cycle that is more personalized—allowing each on-line donor to choose when he or she receives an on-line solicitation. After a year, the results should be analyzed carefully.

The little things. In this chapter, we've outlined how the small things (like type face and teaser copy) should be tested in direct-mail fund-raising. The same should be done on-line. Try to test four factors such as:

1) Does a flashing GIVE icon on the home page draw more traffic to your giving area and improve on-line giving results?

2) What kind of storytelling improves results on-line—something interactive like a quick survey or something multimedia like audio or video? Test different storytelling leading to the on-line reply form.

3) What graphics, colors, font sizes, and font types improve on-line fund-raising results?

4) Can an e-mail follow up after an on-line gift is made improve the future giving pattern for an on-line donor?

Why Did You Just Read This Book?

13 Reasons Direct Response Fund Raising Is So Effective

DAVID LOVE

You have just read a whole book about direct response, and I want to ask a provocative question: *Why?* What is it about direct response that inspired you to read a whole book about it?

Perhaps, like me, you are simply in love with direct response. You love it because it makes you money, it finds and keeps your donors, and it is predictable. My love affair with direct response led me to produce a list of 13 reasons why direct response is at the core of most successful fund-raising programs in the world. Along the way, you'll revisit a few rules that make direct response work and you'll see some exciting, and not so exciting, examples of direct response.

Dawn of Direct Response

But first, I want to take you back thousands of years. Imagine . . .

It's around noon and a small group of men, women, and children dressed in roughly sewn hides is huddled around a smoky campfire somewhere in the wilderness of northern Canada. It's the middle of June and with their constant swatting and cursing, it seems that all these people do is try to fend off dense swarms of voracious bugs.

A young man comes from the woods and joins the group around the fire. The group stares at him in disbelief. The flies aren't bothering him. They fly around him but they don't land or bite.

One man asks, "How come you no have flies around you? Look at rest of us in clouds of bugs."

The young man shrugs sheepishly and says: "The flies used to bother me too. But this morning I fell asleep in some rich green grass by the river, and since then the flies stay away."

Within minutes, everyone around the fire visits the patch of grass and rubs their skin with the fresh green plants. And much to their amazement and delight, the flies stop biting them too.

From then on, the little group carried with them a generous supply of the grass and constantly was on the lookout for a fresh supply.

Many years later we could tell them they just discovered one of the properties of citronella. But what has direct response got to do with a group of hunter-gatherers and their discovery of citronella?

This story is a reminder that direct response has been with us a long time. It's been around so long because at its core, direct response is about action. It's about offering a solution to a problem. It's about changing behavior and immediately improving our lives.

One of the masters of direct response, David Oglivy, in his book *Ogilvy on Advertising*, used this example to illustrate what was different about direct response.

What follows are 13 reasons why direct response is so effective. In each case, you will take a look at an example drawn from the nonprofit world. But before we look at the 13 reasons, let's start with one of the three direct-response rules that provide the groundwork for the subsequent reasons.

Rule #1: ADI(P)A

I am sure you are familiar with this rule, but you can never hear it often enough. These four (and sometimes five) words are at the core of every successful direct response proposition:

> A = attention
> D = desire
> I = interest
> (P) = proof
> A = action

The fourth word, proof, is required if the offer needs some additional support. It is preferable to have such a strong offer that proof is not needed.

In our short story, no one needs proof. The young man gets everyone's attention in a hurry and then creates a strong desire to be like him—bug free! His story of taking a nap in the long grass piques interest and leads the other people to try the grass for themselves.

If you follow the ADI(P)A formula, you will craft a compelling direct-response proposition. To see how well you do, look at your most recent direct-response campaign to get new donors. How does it rate according to our formula?

If you look at any of the classic pieces that have been used time and time again to acquire new donors, you will see that the ADI(P)A formula is at the core of an effective direct response offer.

Nature Conservancy Acquisition Control:
An Example of ADI(P)A at Work

The Nature Conservancy in the United States has used a classic direct-mail acquisition piece for many years.

Take a moment to look at the outer envelope. (See Exhibit 7.1.) (Get's your attention, doesn't it?)

Now let's look at the 13 reasons direct response is so effective.

EXHIBIT 7.1   The Nature Conservancy Acquisition Control: An Example of ADI(P)A at Work

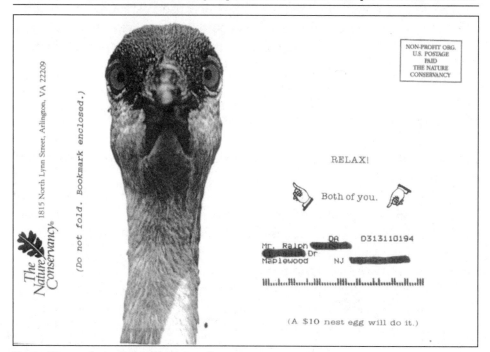

Used with permission from The Nature Conservancy.

Reason 1: Direct Response Is Simple

Direct response is just people talking with each other—for the benefit of both. At a time when you hear so much about how difficult or confusing fund-raising is, direct response remains what it always has been: a simple, personal, one-on-one proposition that leads to action.

Perhaps it is the call to action that makes it so simple. If you want your donors to write you a check right after reading your proposition, you can't afford to be complicated.

Monteverde Rainforest Ad in EQUINOX for the World Wildlife Fund of Canada: An Example of Effective Simplicity

An excellent example of simplicity is the full-page ad from the World Wildlife Fund (WWF) of Canada. (See Exhibit 7.2.) At a time when every media outlet in Canada was talking about the destruction of tropical rain-forest (*Time* magazine even put the issue on the front cover!), WWF Canada invited those concerned about the disappearance of the rain forest to save an acre of it for $25. The ad ran in a widely circulated Canadian magazine and was supported by an editorial and by a 12-page feature article in the same issue.

The response was outstanding. Why? Because WWF Canada made it simple to save tropical rain forest. You could buy an acre of it! And it cost about as much as a case of beer! Finally, that old direct-response classic—the bottom right-hand coupon—makes it easy to respond.

Reason 2: Direct Response Is Measurable

We try so many different things to raise money that sometimes we're not sure if we actually getting anywhere.

With direct response, there is no need to worry about whether your project is a success or failure. You will find out—and usually quickly. This wonderful trait of direct response—direct results—is also a tad humbling.

You can create all sorts of reasons why a certain approach is good. A fund-raising favorite is "long-term cultivation." What you do today will pay off in a few months. While this is certainly true of lots of terrific fund-raising practices, especially in the field of major gifts, if you are involved in direct response, you are allowed no such luxury. You either raise money or you don't.

EXHIBIT 7.2   Monteverde Rainforest Ad in EQUINOX for the World Wildlife Fund of Canada: An Example of Effective Simplicity

WE ARE JUST 8,000 ACRES AWAY FROM SAVING ONE OF THE LAST REMAINING CENTRAL AMERICAN RAINFORESTS

Every $25 donation buys one more acre. And helps protect the Monteverde Nature Reserve in Costa Rica, *forever!*

Walking in the Reserve for only 10 kilometers, you would see as many different types of forest and species as you would hiking all the way from Nova Scotia to British Columbia.

Sadly, if the hundreds of different trees, flowers, ferns, vines, herbs, lichens, mosses, butterflies, birds and other wildlife thriving here lose their home, *they will not be the only victims.* You have as much to lose as they do:

Half the *crops which feed the world* depend on these forests. One quarter of our prescription drugs have active ingredients found in tropical plants. For example, substances contained in the Rosy Periwinkle are *increasing the remission rate for childhood leukaemia*—from 20% in 1969 to over 90% in 1987!

Happily, the Monteverde Nature Reserve is rapidly growing. Through the combined efforts of the Monteverde Conservation League, Equinox Magazine, World Wildlife Fund and the generosity of concerned Canadians, 22,000 acres are safe.

But despite the fact that the Reserve has more than doubled in size, we're not quite "out of the woods" yet.

And that's why we need your help

Only 8,000 acres are left. Every $25 donation you make buys another acre. In recognition of your support, we'll send you an Honorary Deed in your name, for the acres you save.

You may also want to reserve acres on behalf of your family and friends: Honour the birth of a child, celebrate a birthday or anniversary...or mark any special occasion by giving a gift that lasts forever. The Honorary Deed, and what it stands for, will be a keepsake they will certainly treasure.

Display your Honorary Deed with pride

Your $25 can save this acre

50 acres of vital tropical forest disappear every minute of every day! You have an opportunity to help save one of the last remaining Central American rainforests.

To contribute, simply complete and return this coupon (or a facsimile), with your cheque, money order or credit card information to:

World Wildlife Fund
60 St. Clair Avenue East, Suite 201
Toronto, Ontario M4T 1N5
(416) 973-8173

I understand this money will be used exclusively for the preservation of the Monteverde Nature Reserve in Costa Rica, not for administration or office expenses.

I would like to preserve:

☐ 200 Acres ☐ 100 Acres ☐ 40 Acres
☐ 20 Acres ☐ 10 Acres ☐ 4 Acres
☐ 2 Acres ☐ 1 Acre ☐ Other ____
At $25 per acre, my total donation is: $ ____

Name ____
Address ____
Apt. ____ City ____
Province ____ Postal Code ____
This is a gift. Please issue the Honorary Deed in the name of: ____

☐ Cheque enclosed. ☐ Money order enclosed.
☐ VISA ☐ MasterCard

Card # ____
Expiry date ____
Signature ____

☐ Please send me an action checklist of what's being done to preserve this and other Reserves

An official tax receipt will be sent for all donations of $10 or more.

Sometimes you think you have created the best direct-response piece ever only to be taught by results that what you think doesn't matter. It doesn't even matter what your audience thinks about it. What matters is what your audience *does* with it.

Exhibit 7.3 is a mailing done for a political party in Canada.

Federal New Democratic Party: What You Think Doesn't Matter— Results Matter!

In 1990 the Federal New Democratic Party was an opposition party in the Canadian Federal landscape. It wanted to send out a piece of political fund-raising that showed its supporters what could be accomplished if the party came to power.

The package's letter began with an imaginary excerpt from the Parliamentary Hansard—the official, word-by-word record of parliamentary proceedings. The imaginary excerpt recounted a speech made by the prime minister—the current opposition leader for the New Democratic Party.

The look, design, and cadence of the imaginary Hansard was taken from the official one. Mike Johnston, then a direct-response consultant for the Federal New Democratic Party, met with party officials to review the direct-mail package. He remembers the scene.

> We walked to a window overlooking Parliament. The staff told me how much they loved the package, especially the Hansard approach, and I admitted I like the package as well. I should have known that to have both the client and consultant pleased with a direct-mail package is sometimes worrisome.
>
> There needs to be a dynamic tension in creating packages, and we shouldn't create direct response to please the egos involved. It should only be focused on the donor. The mailing went on to do poorly—much to the dismay of the political staff who had loved the package.

Reason 3: Direct Response Is Personal

This is one of the most misunderstood things about direct response, especially direct mail. People call it a mass medium that does not take into account the individual. Nothing could be further from the truth.

When a direct-mail piece comes in a person's mail, that person is in complete control of the rest of the transaction—if there is to be one! First,

**EXHIBIT 7.3   The Federal New Democratic Party: What You Think Doesn't Matter—
Results Matter!**

From the House of Commons in the year 1993:

Right Hon. Audrey McLaughlin (Prime Minister): Mr. Speaker, I
hope my honourable opponent realizes that the New Democrat
government is simply implementing the policies that Canadians
voted for in last year's election. The people of Canada have
given us the mandate to revitalize and reinvest in this country.

Some Hon. Members: Here, Here!

Hon. Brian Mulroney (Leader of the Opposition): Mr. Speaker, the
Conservative Party of Canada is firmly against this government's
decisions to reinvest in our national railways, to disassemble
the Mexico-US-Canada Free Trade deal, and to eliminate the GST.

                                        Parliamentary Hansard

Dear Friend:

     I want to see the day when I can read about the above
encounter -- a time when we'll rebuild the Canada you and I
believe in.

     That's why I'd like to tell you about the political leader
who's capturing the imagination of people like you and me across
Canada.

     Audrey McLaughlin, leader of the federal New Democrats.

     She's brought a fresh, new perspective to the Canadian
political scene - a caring, compassionate leader who believes in
open and honest government.

     And what's more, she's got what it takes to win the next
election!

     Her honest and open style of politics is catching on. In a
recent Angus Reid-Southam News poll, Audrey had the highest
approval rating of any federal leader.

     I'm writing to you today to invite you to join Audrey's
winning team.
                                        (over please)

                600–280 Albert Street, Ottawa K1P 5G8

Used with permission from New Democratic Party of Canada.

the person either opens it or does not. The person can even decide to wait. After opening it, the person can respond or not. There is no pressure. The offer either moves the person in the comfort of his or her own home and on his or her terms or it doesn't. What could be more personal than that?

Because it's personal, direct response can also be intimate. When reading a good direct-mail piece, a person is having a personal conversation with an interesting individual who is talking not to everyone but to him or her—right now.

Covenant House: The Personal Approach

Covenant House is supremely adept at finding a tone and approach that is personal and very emotional. Many fund-raising professionals would flinch if they thought to approach a letter or appeal like the text that follows:

> A lady should never get this dirty, she said.
> She stood there with a quiet, proud dignity. She was *incomparably* dirty—her face and hands smeared, her clothes torn and soiled. The lady was 11.
> My brothers are hungry, she said. The two little boys she hugged protectively were 8 and 9. They were three of the most beautiful children I'd ever seen.
> Our parents beat us a lot, she said. . . .

The letter's language is personal and very effective.

Reason 4: Direct Response Is Smart

One of the great things about direct response is that it learns as fund-raisers go along. Because the response is immediate, fund-raisers can continue to refine the offer until it is reaches its maximum return on investment (ROI). And then they can try a completely different approach to see if they can get an even better ROI.

This process is at the core of healthy acquisition programs that start with an established control and then work to beat that control. Of course, once the new control is established, fund-raisers work to beat that one.

The ability of direct response to learn is at the heart of successful telemarketing campaigns where, from the audience, fund-raisers discover things that improve the offer and then change things to improve the response.

It is this ability to learn continually from actions that makes direct response so smart. This element is what leads some practitioners to talk about the *science* of direct response.

Reason 5: Direct Response Is Testable

Not only is direct response smart, it is testable. We all have treasured opinions about what works and what doesn't. Once again, because direct response is quick and measurable, we can look at how people respond to two different offers.

People have written whole books about testing. In a typical direct-mail piece, different outer envelopes, different letters, different inserts, different response coupons, different donation amounts, and, as the following example shows, different business reply envelopes can be tested.

But which of all of these elements should be tested? The answer is usually the element that has the best opportunity to make a mailing more profitable.

Proof That You Need to Keep It Simple:
"Your Stamp Can Help Us More"

For years, nonprofit organizations in Canada included a statement in the top left-hand corner of their return envelope. The envelope would tell prospective donors that "BY INCLUDING A STAMP YOU'LL BE SAVING US MONEY" or some other similar cost-cutting statement.

It was always assumed that this statement would increase response and save organizations money in return postage. Stephen Thomas, a senior direct-mail in Canada, tested this assumption (see Exhibit 7.4) and found that including a message on a postage paid envelope would *reduce* response. Stephen was able to strip away the clutter of text and keep the reply envelope simple—and more effective.

Rule #2 = KISS

Let's take a break from the 13 reasons direct response is so effective and go back to our next basic direct response rule: KISS, or "keep it simple stupid." Because the "testability" of direct response is so powerful, users can

EXHIBIT 7.4   Never Take Anything for Granted

Your stamp here will help us save money

MAIL ⟩ POSTE
Canada Post Corporation
Société canadienne des postes
Postage paid   Port payé
If mailed in Canada   si posté au Canada
Business Reply   Réponse d'affaires
0398770100   01

Society for Two-Headed Animals
Box 500 Station A
Ottawa, Ontario
K3Y 2X5

get carried away with it and can make direct response complicated. At these moments, you need to remember the KISS rule:

K = Keep
 I = It
S = Simple
S = Stupid

My favorite of these words is the last one. Often it is the desire to show off one's brilliance that gets fund-raisers into trouble in direct response. Their well-educated brain takes them away from the essence of a simple direct-response transaction. You talk; I act. It's that simple.

George Orwell, a longtime advocate of simplicity over obfuscation, provides the best examples of KISS. In his wonderful essay, *Politics and the English Language,* written in 1946, he offered his own list of six questions that every writer (direct-response fund-raiser in this case) should ask him- or herself:

1. What am I trying to say?
2. What words will express it?
3. What image or idiom will make it clearer?
4. Is the image fresh enough to make the effect?
5. Could I put it more shortly?
6. Have I said anything that is avoidably ugly?

And Orwell offered a list of six directives that would challenge any fund-raising writer even more:

1. Never use a metaphor, simile, or other figure of speech that you are used to seeing in print.
2. Never use a long word where a short one will do.
3. If it is possible to cut a word out, always cut it out.
4. Never use the passive voice when you can use the active voice.
5. Never use a foreign phrase, a scientific word, or a jargon word if you can think of an everyday English equivalent.
6. Break any of these rules sooner than say anything outright barbarous.

In his essay, Orwell is challenging us to not become lazy writers. We need to look carefully at everything we've written and, most likely, write it again, and again. He went on to say the following about modern writing, but he could have been talking about direct-response fund-raising prose: "Modern writing at its worst does not consist of picking out words for the sake of their meaning and inventing images to make the meaning clearer. It consists of gumming together long strips of words, which have already been set in order by someone else, and making the results presentable by sheer humbug."

Sound familiar? I thought so. Effective direct response needs effective use of words, and there's no better place to learn than with George Orwell.

Having engraved the second rule into your head, let's look at four more reasons direct response is at the core of so many brilliant fund-raising programs.

Reason 6: Direct Response Is Intelligent

In July 1999 David Ogilvy died at the ripe old age of 88. He was a brilliant and inspired advocate of direct response, and on a number of occasions he referred to it as his "secret weapon" in sales.

It was direct response's ability to make use of research and knowledge that placed it at the top of Ogilvy's preferred methods of selling. Those who worked in his agencies around the world were familiar with this famous Ogilvyism: "We prefer the discipline of knowledge to the anarchy of ignorance. We pursue knowledge the way a pig pursues truffles."

Good direct response is based on research and knowledge, not on bias and opinion. Frankly, there is no excuse for not doing your homework, because the more you know about your offer and your donor, the more effective you will be in raising money for your mission.

Arthritis Society of Alberta: Intelligent Direct Response

The Arthritis Society of Alberta conducted a survey of its donors in 1998. The results of that survey indicated that individuals supported the organization because of their personal connection to arthritis (they had it or a friend or family member struggled with it) and they believed that arthritis was a complicated and difficult disorder that demanded a wide range of initiatives to help individuals (e.g., they thought that the Arthritis Society should pursue a multitiered approach: research, support programs, and education).

Knowing what their donors wanted, the Arthritis Society of Alberta crafted an annual renewal package (see Exhibit 7.5) that tried to communicate this multitiered approach. A letter written by Herrat Zahner, a senior volunteer for the society, outlined a solicitation approach indicated by the survey results.

The results were staggering. The response for this annual renewal package improved by over 10 percent from past renewal mailings (coming in at an impressive 34 percent), and it had to do, in part, to the ability of direct-response fund-raising to be intelligent—learning and changing according to the needs and responses of individuals.

Reason 7: Direct Response Is Practical

Direct response is about results. Period. Results are the only valid measure of a direct-response offer. In direct response, everything, including creativity, plays second fiddle to results. It may look great to put a coupon in the middle of a page, but it simply won't work!

This practical approach allows practitioners of direct response to ensure that all elements of the offer—the audience, the design, the copy, and the response device—work toward the single end: results. And what better criteria can there be for evaluating an offer we make to an audience?

What Happens When You Don't Keep It Simple

The World Wildlife Fund of Canada created a newspaper ad with the coupon in the middle of the page. (See Exhibit 7.6.) It bombed.

EXHIBIT 7.5   The Arthritis Society of Alberta: Intelligent Direct Response

Mrs. Jane Sample
123 Main St.
Anytown, Anywhere

Dear Mrs. Sample,

Isn't it the best thing in the world when you get a love-filled letter from your grandchild, a sister, or your mother?

I loved writing letters to my family -- to my children, brothers and sisters -- everyone. I kept in touch with everybody and passed on information. I was proud of my role as the family communicator.

But suddenly, nine years ago... I couldn't write anymore. My fingers were swollen as big as sausages and the pain from picking up a pen was unbearable.

It was a frightening morning when I woke up and discovered I couldn't move -- I couldn't even get myself out of bed!

Arthritis now stood between me and my family.

I'm writing to you today to tell you how The Arthritis Society helped me become the family communicator again and how your renewed support will allow The Arthritis Society to help many other people like they've helped me.

~~That's why I've sent you one of my dearest treasures along with~~ **this letter**: a <u>foam rubber grip</u> that's just like the one that I have on my pen.

You may wonder how it could mean so much to me, but when you've read my whole story, you'll understand.

When my arthritis first struck, I was living my typically busy life: coordinating a committee for a women's conference; looking after my
mother-in-law; and, volunteering my time for a major charity.

I knew something was terribly wrong, when my husband Mike and I were to drive to one of his functions in Red Deer. I love to drive, but when I got behind the steering wheel, I realized I couldn't hold on. It was just too painful.

...1

Used with permission from The Arthritis Society, Alberta and NWT Division.

EXHIBIT 7.6 Full-Page Beluga Whale Ad: What Happens When You Don't Keep It Simple!

the Beluga (White) whale

GONE?

TO: World Wildlife Fund Canada
60 St. Clair Avenue East, Suite 201
Toronto, Ontario M4T1N5

I enclose $25 $100 $1000 $_____ (other)
I understand my entire donation goes directly to field
work for Beluga Whales. Not for any administrative
purposes.

Name _____

Address _____

City _____ Prov. _____ P. Code _____

Please send me: ☐ An action check-list of what's being done
to save the Beluga Whale
☐ The WWF Canada quarterly newspaper
☐ An official tax receipt
☐ Your bequest brochure

Beluga, the white whale. One small population of these graceful creatures lives in our St. Lawrence River. Thirty-five years ago, they numbered in the thousands. Today's estimate–about 300.

Belugas are warm-blooded. They bear live young, and nurse them with milk. They appear to be very intelligent, social animals. In some ways, they are remarkably like humans. And we are their worst enemy.

St. Lawrence Belugas are absolutely dependent on rivermouths for feeding and rearing their young. And more and more, we pollute those areas with toxic chemicals. And interfere with water levels and temperatures. And frighten the whales away with power-boats.

Wildlife species can provide priceless lessons in medicine, and technology. Already whales have given us the concept of sonar, and insights into our own body-temperature controls. Who knows how they might help us in the future. If they're still here, that is.

At least half the world's Belugas live in Canada. So we have a special responsibility. Fortunately, they are still fairly abundant in the Arctic. But it will be all we can do to save the St. Lawrence Beluga.

World Wildlife Fund is supporting plans for a marine park to protect the St. Lawrence Beluga, and conducting studies with the Inuit into Arctic populations. But unless we can learn more, and do more, we cannot rest easy–even about the Arctic Belugas.

You can help. With a donation to World Wildlife Fund. Each $25 buys a set of posters on how to avoid disturbing whales. $100 gets 150 litres of fuel for Arctic aerial surveys. $1000 provides a boat for field biologists.

Please send $25 or more (or less) to Project Beluga, World Wildlife Fund.

WWF

 WORLD WILDLIFE FUND (CANADA)
FONDS MONDIAL POUR LA NATURE (CANADA)

60 ST. CLAIR AVENUE EAST, SUITE 201
TORONTO, ONT. M4T 1N5. (416) 923-8173

Used with permission from World Wildlife Fund Canada, 245 Eglinton Avenue East, Suite 410, Toronto, ON, Canada M4P 3J1, www.wwf.com.

Reason 8: Direct Response Is Cost Effective

Because the response is immediate, it is easy to calculate the return on investment for a direct-response piece. In the charitable sector, cost per donor is examined constantly—how much does it cost to recruit a donor through any number of direct-response media?

Since how that donor responds to various offers over time can be tracked, how much a certain donor is worth to an organization can be calculated.

Like testing, there are whole books written about long-term value. But also like testing, at its core it is simple. The immediacy of direct response and the control of the variables that allow users to determine how cost effective direct-response activities are.

At a time when accountability matters more and more to donors, the cost-effectiveness of direct response will ensure that it will remain a crucial element of a mature fund-raising program.

Reason 9: Direct Response Is Everywhere

We are bombarded by direct response all the time. Just look at the environmental movement in the United States and Canada. There are literally thousands of organizations talking to potential donors and members about the need to be environmentally responsible.

This means that offers are being made all the time that are wrestling with the best ways to invite new donors and encourage current ones to contribute to their cause. Fund-raisers can see all these offers by joining appropriate organizations with a minimum contribution. And by watching the mail and reading about direct marketing, it is clear which ideas and offers are working.

Finally, best of all, after seeing what is working, fund-raisers can steal it and use it themselves. Because direct response is everywhere, it submits itself to a process of continuous improvement. And because the results are continually in the public domain, fund-raisers can learn from others and use their success to become more successful. (Of course, then others will use that success to be more successful too!)

Easter Seals Society of Ontario: Piggybacking on the Success of Others

This example comes from Mike Johnston, a fund-raising consultant in Toronto and the editor of this book. Mike says:

The Easter Seal Society of Ontario needed to improve the recapture rates for its lapsed donors (those who hadn't given for 18 to 36 months). I was reading through Con Squires's excellent newsletter, *The Direct Response Donor,* when I saw a letter that Con had written for an American organization. Con had mentioned that this letter had proven to be highly successful. The two organizations have different missions, but I thought the very personal approach would be directly adaptable.

The letter was hard hitting but fair (see Exhibit 7.7a), and I thought I'd extract the structure and approach of the letter for the Easter Seals Society of Ontario. I paraphrased the lead from Con's letter: "If you were writing to a good friend who hadn't answered your letters, would you feel a bit awkward and not know just what to say . . .?"

The letter went on to use the same structure as Con's letter (see Exhibit 7.7b), outlining a number of ways a renewed gift would help children with physical disabilities. I ended with another paraphrase of his ending: "So please don't be upset if I worry when I don't hear from you. I hope you'll renew your much-missed help now! Good friends don't grow on trees, and friends who care enough as you have done are rare indeed!"

The letter was a runaway success and had an amazing 8 percent response to lapsed donors. By borrowing some of the language from Con's example, and with proof that this approach had worked before, I was able to persuade Easter Seal fund-raising staff that this letter was worth testing. Without past evidence that it had worked, this letter would never have been mailed.

Mike's example shows that people can borrow from the successes of others to ensure that their own direct-response fund-raising efforts are profitable. Do it. Copy, borrow, and steal where you can!

Rule #3: Features and Benefits

The last direct-response rule is about features and benefits. Like ADI(P)A and KISS, this rule is at the core of any direct-response offer.

To show how features and benefits work, we are going to use the example of the number-10 wooden pencil with an eraser on the top.

Mighty Pencil: An Example of Features of Benefits

We define features and benefits by saying a feature of the pencil is "What It Does" and a benefit of this pencil is "What It Does for ME!" This crucial

EXHIBIT 7.7A   Borrow Someone's Good Work

The National Copy Clinic

SAMPLE

Mr. John D. Sample
22 Sample Street
Sample, MA. 02166

Dear Mr. Sample:

If you were writing to a good friend you'd been out of touch with for a while, would you feel a bit awkward and not know just what to say?

That's how I feel now, because I haven't heard from you since June, 1985 when the Hospital got your last generous gift of $000. And we've missed you.

Some people might look around a multi-million dollar hospital like this one and say, well, what's one gift of $000 more or less? Not me! I know better.

I look at a doctor or nurse using up-to-date equipment to care for a sick elderly patient and I know gifts of $000 bought that equipment.

I see a teddy bear in the arms of a sleeping girl in our intensive care unit and I know gifts of $000 bought that teddy bear for lots of sick boys and girls!

I walk down well-lit corridors, smell clean, fresh air, see patients eating meals that both look and taste good — and I know gifts of $000 make such things happen every day.

So please don't be upset if I worry when I don't hear from you. Or hope you'll renew your much-missed help now! Good friends don't grow on trees, and friends who care enough to help as you have done are rare indeed!

I hope to hear from you soon, Mr. Sample.

Sincerely,
Signer
Position

P.S. Don't forget to send the enclosed slip with your gift so we can put the name of Mr. John D. Sample on our 1992 Honor Roll in our lobby. It will be GREAT to see your name there again!

22 Lake Avenue, Auburndale, MA 02166 • (617)332-2746

Used with permission from The National Copy Clinic.

EXHIBIT 7.7B   Easter Seals Society of Ontario: Piggybacking on the Success of Others

---

Serving children with physical disabilities since 1922

The Easter Seal Society
250 Ferrand Drive. Suite 200
Don Mills. Ontario M3C 3P2

Mr. John H. Sample
990 Roselawn Avenue   xx21 (J)
Toronto, Ontario
M6B 1C1

Dear Mr. Sample,

If you were writing to a good friend who hadn't answered your letters, would you feel a bit awkward and not know just what to say?

That's how I feel now, because I haven't heard from you since that important letter I sent you over one month ago. In fact, I haven't heard from you since March 19, 1993 when The Easter Seal Society received your generous gift of $10.00.

Some people might not realize how important each and every contribution is to the more than 8,000 children with physical disabilities served by The Easter Seal Society. Not me. I know better.

I look at a speech therapist using up-to-date computer equipment to help a severely disabled boy to tell the world what he loves about the Blue Jays and I know your gift of $10.00 helped purchase that equipment.

I see a smile on the face of a sleeping girl who has been on her first hike at camp because of an electric wheelchair I know your $10.00 helped provide.

I see the parent support, the hundreds of children with physical disabilities integrated into school programs, the thousands of nurse home visits, and the fun-filled camping holidays -- and I know gifts of $10.00 make such things happen every day.

So please don't be upset if I worry when I don't hear from you. Or hope you'll renew your much-missed help now! Good friends don't grow on trees, and friends who care enough as you have done are rare indeed!

I hope to hear from you soon, Mr. Sample.

Sincerely,

Peter Ely
Executive Director

P.S. Please accept and use the 1994 seals I've enclosed. And, if you send your gift by May 31st, we will send you a copy of the premiere edition of our *Kids! First* newsletter.

P.S.S. If you have recently sent in your gift, thank you, your commitment to the children is appreciated.

Used with permission from The Easter Seal Society, Ontario Division.

distinction is vital to all direct-response offers that must be about benefits as well as features.

Let's consider the pencil for a moment. One of its features is that it is made out of wood. Benefits that come from this feature are:

- You could start a fire with it.
- You can make a boat out of it.
- You can resharpen it.

Another feature of a pencil is that it is sharp. Some benefits are:

- You can draw and write beautifully with it.
- You can use it as a weapon.
- You can use it as a thumb tack.
- You can use it to poke holes in a plastic bag that was placed over your head.

Another feature is that it has an eraser on the end. Some benefits are:

- You can correct your mistakes.
- You can smudge your drawings.

For every feature of the pencil (it is light, it is long, it is yellow), there are benefits. The same thinking is behind direct-response offers. It is not enough to tell prospective donors what an organization does. Donors must be told what the organization does for them.

Now let's look at the four final traits that make direct response so important and useful for fund-raisers.

Reason 10: Direct Response Is a Master of Disguise

Direct response comes in many forms: a newspaper ad, a brochure, a letter, a phone call, a person at your door, a TV show, a radio program, an Internet site, a billboard, a movie screen, a dirigible, and many more.

All of these media can be used to urge donors to take action immediately. Obviously, some are better than others at generating immediate response. Currently many organizations are effectively using TV to generate response. What was once thought a passive medium can become active. Those using TV well have garnered excellent results.

But no matter what clothes are put on direct response, the principles that make it work remain the same: ADI(P)A, KISS, and Features and Benefits.

DRTV: Amnesty International Canada

Once again, we come back to Amnesty International Canada. Two years ago Amnesty Canada launched its direct-response television spots, which included emotional stories told by TV and movie celebrities like Martin Sheen. The approach can seem like a documentary mixed with an evangelical fervor, somewhat like on-air preachers. (See Exhibit 7.8.) The host, Martin Sheen, is a fund-raiser's dream come true. He is direct, is persuasive, and doesn't miss the chance to ask the watcher to pick up the phone and donate.

The program has been so effective that Amnesty Canada is now able to take some of the overbudget fund-raising results from the DRTV program and put them into other areas of its work.

Reason 11: Direct Response Is Empathetic

Direct response is not about the seller. It is about the buyer. What does the donor want? How does the donor feel? Direct marketing is not about the organization. It's about how the donor can interact with the organization and its mission.

Some charities today are sending donors "welcome books," a special communication that encourages donors to customize their relationship with the charity. And a staple of many of these books is a short donor survey.

Direct response is rooted in the principles that fund-raisers can't know too much about their donors and that the more that is learned about them, the more empathetic fund-raisers are, the better the organization will do.

Welcome Book—the Canadian Cancer Society

The best welcome book includes a donor survey. The Canadian Cancer Society has created a succinct and successful welcome package that incorporates a donor upgrade, survey, and explanation on how a donor can become more involved—all on one $8\frac{1}{2} \times 14$ sheet of paper. So who says they have to be big and bulky? (See Exhibit 7.9.)

EXHIBIT 7.8   Amnesty International Canada-DRTV

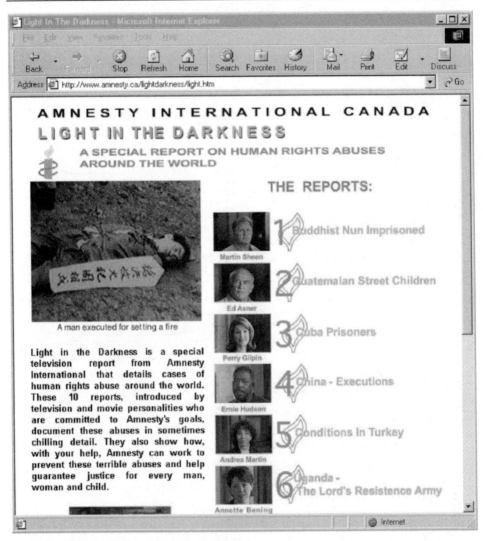

Used with permission from Amnesty International Canada.

Reason 12: Direct Response Is a Problem Solver

Because it moves a person to action, direct response is about solutions, not about problems. Direct response does not bombard readers with so many facts and issues and concerns that they become paralyzed with inaction.

Rather, direct response clearly presents a pressing problem and then proposes an effective solution.

EXHIBIT 7.9   The Canadian Cancer Society Welcome Book

CAN YOU INTRODUCE A FRIEND TO US?

You might know a family member, friend or colleague who might also want to help fund cancer research and support programs. If you do, please add their name and contact information directly below. Of course, they will be under no obligation to support the Canadian Cancer Society, but we hope they will because we need all the help we can get against cancer!

Please fill in the names and contact information and put this form into the return envelope I included for you.

NAME

ADDRESS

POSTAL CODE

TELEPHONE

NAME

ADDRESS

POSTAL CODE

TELEPHONE

It's our 60th Anniversary! It's a special time that offers us a valuable opportunity to take stock of our mission and our services. As we look to the past, we can see our progress -- helping more Manitobans survive cancer and return to a normal life - while at the same time getting closer to an ultimate cure.

As we look to the future, it is clear that the support of people like you will be essential to our future success. For these reasons, we hope you will set aside a few minutes to answer the questions on the attached survey and then return the form to us. We look forward to receiving your response.

1. Which of the following do you feel is the most important of the Canadian Cancer Society's work? Please check only one:

    ( ) Health promotion and awareness
    ( ) Cancer research
    ( ) Patient services
    ( ) Advocacy

2. Volunteers are a vital part of providing support to Manitobans struggling with cancer and their families. If you don't volunteer with the Canadian Cancer Society is there something you'd like to do with us?

    _____

3. Remembering the Canadian Cancer Society in your will can be the best way to make a difference to those struggling against cancer after you're gone. Have you included the Canadian Cancer Society in your will already?   ( ) YES   ( ) NO .

    If not, would you like more information on making a bequest through your will or other ways to leave a lasting gift?   ( ) YES   ( ) NO

4. What is your gender?   ( ) M   ( ) F

5. What is your age?   ( ) Under 35 ( ) 35-44
                        ( ) 45-55   ( ) 55-64
                        ( ) 65-74   ( ) 75+

6. What is your home telephone number?

    _____

7. Do you have a personal story of cancer survival you would be willing to share with other Society supporters?
    ( ) NO   ( ) YES
    ( ) If YES, then please include your contact number
    ( ) I've included an extra sheet of paper explaining my story.

WE NEED YOUR REGULAR SUPPORT

Research is, by necessity, a long-term undertaking. That's why your regular support is particularly valuable. Because it enables us to plan very effectively for the future. Our monthly supported plan, PARTNERS IN HOPE, lets you help us plan for a future that will include a cure for cancer.

By joining PARTNERS IN HOPE PLAN, you allow us to make automatic withdrawals from your chequing account every month. For as little as the cost of a restaurant lunch once a month, we can increase our funding to vital medical research and expand our services to the increasing number of Manitobans battling cancer.

PARTNERS IN HOPE PLAN

I want to become a PARTNERS IN HOPE Plan monthly supporter of the Canadian Cancer Society. On the 15th or 30th day of each month (circle one), I/we authorize you to receive from the account specified on my cheque (attached) the following special contribution:

❑ $30   ❑ $20   ❑ $10   ❑ Other $ _____

Please enclose a void cheque with this form. Subsequent donations will be deducted from your account. And, at the end of the calendar year, we'll send you a tax-receipt for the total of your year's contribution.
IF YOU WANT TO MAKE ANY CHANGE to your monthly contribution simply call (204) 774-7483 (Wpg.) and ask for our Director of Revenue Development and Communications.

❑ My voided cheque is enclosed

Bank: _____

Branch: _____

Account #: _____

❑ I prefer to contribute using:
   ❑ VISA   ❑ MasterCard   ❑ AMEX

Card Number: _____

Expiry Date: _____

Today's Date: _____

Signature: _____

Signature: _____
If two signatures are required on this account, please include both.

When you join the PARTNERS IN HOPE Plan we'll send you a cookbook!

Used with permission from Canadian Cancer Society—Manitoba Division.

In a blizzard of offers from for profits and not-for-profits, the ones that stand out are those that compellingly paint a picture and then let readers (or viewers or listeners) complete the picture.

Like a good story, direct response has a beginning, a middle, and an end. And the end brings satisfaction because the last element of a direct-response transaction is a measurable, tangible, important action on the part of the audience.

Emergency Piece: The Beginning, Middle, and End of a Classic Red Cross Package

Exhibit 7.10 presents a classic Red Cross emergency piece where people can take immediate action on a crucial issue.

Reason 13: Direct Response Is a Loyalty Builder

I've saved the best for last. Because direct response is all about donor action, it allows fund-raisers to continually delight your best customers. It is through these actions that substantial donor loyalty can be built.

EXHIBIT 7.10   Manitoba Flood Emergency Piece: The Beginning, Middle, and End of a Classic Red Cross Package

---

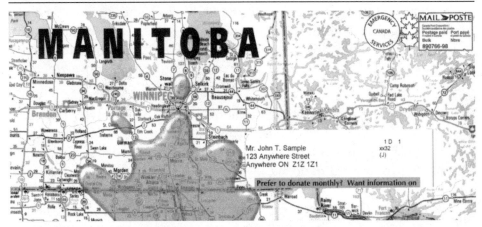

Used with permission from Canadian Red Cross Package.

Just as in the for-profit world, in the not-for-profit world loyal customers are the most important customers. These are the women and men who will work tirelessly with the organization to accomplish a shared mission.

The ability to build loyalty in donors through direct response is at the core of some of the most profitable customers to charities—monthly donors.

Also, if circumstances permit, loyal donors will become major donors to a cause. They may even make a planned gift to the organization work as well. Recent research in the United Kingdom confirms that planned gifts come from those donors who give regular small amounts to offers as they are presented, sometimes over many years.

Conclusion

It's the year 2050, and the Environmental Greenpeace Protection Foundation (EGPF), an amalgam of environmental groups, is gearing up for a major fund-raising campaign. The colonized settlements of Mars have just discovered that the industrial pollutants coming from their planetory plants are threatening the habitat and existence of a newly discovered three-headed, red-furred seal.

The EGPF will raise money through the following methods:

• *A floating door-to-door android.* A mechanical/organic head flies from house to house. The bodiless head can project holographs of the environmental disaster (in real time) via satellite on the person's doorstep. Androids can take payment via any computerized card.

• *Web site.* An on-line visitor to the EGPF Web site downloads a virtual reality game onto a home entertainment system and begins to live through the three heads of the red-furred seal. At the end of this virtual experience, a glowing hovering marker can be tapped and a donation made while the donor stands on the Red Planet.

• *Personalized appeals.* Current donors to the EGPF receive a personalized appeal from their EGPF field contact. When they come home, an "urgent message icon" is blinking at the top of their home mail system. On signing in, here is what happens:

Hello, David. Good to hear from you again. Your special project on the grizzly bear is going really well. You'll get pictures and results from the field next week.

Thanks for your prompt response. But I know you will want to know about this new emergency.

But before I tell you, today was the day of your big presentation at work, wasn't it? How did it go? I'm sure you knocked them out.

Now, about that emergency on Mars. . . .

Though these media seem distant and difficult to imagine, the point is that while the media change, the drivers of direct response will remain the same. The multimedia, virtual, floating messages still use many of the 13 reasons why direct-response fund-raising will remain so effective—even in the year 2050. And the three rules will still apply.

▼ About the CD-ROM

System Requirements

- IBM PC with 100 MHz or faster Pentium® or compatible processor
- Microsoft® Windows 95 or later
- A web browser such as Netscape® Navigator 4.0 or greater, or Microsoft® Internet Explorer 4.0 or greater
- 16 MB RAM
- 16-bit color display monitor with a minimum resolution of 640 x 480
- 4x CD-ROM drive
- RealPlayer® 7.0 or greater
- Sound Blaster 16 or compatible sound card
- Mouse
- Speakers

How to Run the CD-ROM on Your Computer

The CD-ROM is equipped with an **Autorun** program. To run the program, place the CD-ROM into the CD drive of your computer; and a screen will appear on your monitor asking you to click **Start** to begin viewing the CD-ROM.

If you need to start the CD-ROM after quitting, you may do so by one of two methods:

1. Remove the CD-ROM from your computer and begin the process as stated above, or
2. Go to your desktop, open **My Computer** and double click on the **Direct_Response** icon.
3. If the step 2 does not work, open **My Computer**, go to the **CD-ROM Drive**, right click on your mouse, explore the CD-ROM and then double click on **Direct_Response.exe**.

If the program freezes or crashes, your computer may be experiencing problems of insufficient memory allocation. Close all other open programs, then launch and minimize your Web browser before starting the CD-ROM program.

Using the Sample Packages on the CD-ROM

Seeing the Sample Packages

Having pressed **Start** on the opening page of the CD-ROM, you will see a screen containing the **Cover** of the book and a set of **pull-down menus** on the right hand side. This CD-ROM includes not only the samples referred to in the text of the book, but others as well. You may choose to explore the sample packages in one of three ways using the pull-down menus:

- By the *Book Reference* of a package component as it appears in the text of the book. Although the Book Reference number refers to one piece of a sample package, which will be the default document through this search method, the whole package is viewable.
- By *Organization Name*: This menu contains a sub-menu dividing the organization names in alphabetical sections A-D, E-N, O-S, and T-Z. Click on one of these sub-menus to access a given organization name.
- By *Type of Organization*, categorized as Education, Health, Civic, Social/Welfare, or Government.

Click on the search menu of your choice and then click on the sample package you wish to view.

Seeing Exhibit Components

Once on the page of a particular Sample Package you will see the **default component** of the package in the center of the screen, and a series of **package navigation icons** on the left hand side of the screen. Each of these navigation icons represents a particular component in the package: the outer envelope, the letter, the reply envelope, the premium, the insert. Not all packages contain all of these elements, and in these cases the package navigation icon box will be blank.

At the bottom of these icons is an icon to enlarge the size of the item being viewed (it looks like a magnifying glass with a "+" sign in it). This will take you to an enlarged view of the sample package component. The cursor will appear as a small hand when rolled over the component. Pressing and holding the left button on your mouse will allow you to move the component about in the viewing window. If you wish to go back to the standard view of the component, click on the reduction icon on the lower right side of the enlargement screen. (This icon looks like a magnifying glass with a "-" in it.)

Some of the components of the packages, the letter for example, may be two or three pages in length. This will be indicated by the Multiple Page Icons, appearing as numbered icons below the component. To access the other pages of a particular component, click on the numbered icon.

Printing Pages

If you want to print specific pages from the CD-ROM, select **File, Print Sample** from the pull-down menu. This will take you to a standard Windows print dialog box. Be sure your paper size is set to "Letter".

User Assistance

If you need assistance with installation or if you have a damaged disk, please contact Wiley Technical Support at:

T: (212) 850-6753
F: (212) 850-6800 (Attention: Wiley Technical Support)
E: *techhelp@wiley.com*

To place additional order or to request information about other Wiley Products, please call (800) 225-5945.

CD-ROM Contents

Searchable by:

- Book Exhibit Reference
  - 2-3: Sunshine Centre for Seniors—Bird Paintings
  - 2-4: Canadian Diabetes Association Manitoba Div.—Camp Envelope
  - Appendix B: Three-Year Scheduling Document
  - 6-1: Smithsonian NMAI—Membership Appeal 1991, Plain Envelope
  - 6-2: Smithsonian NMAI—Membership Appeal 1991, Mask Envelope
  - 6-3: Smithsonian NMAI—Membership Appeal 1991, Text Envelope

- 6-4: Smithsonian NMAI—Membership Appeal with Name Stickers
- 6-5: AARP Andrus Foundation—Feather/Inkwell Name Stickers, 1998
- 6-6: AARP Andrus Foundation—Puppies and Kittens Name Stickers, 1999
- 6-7: AARP Andrus Foundation—Sun and Moon Name Stickers, 1999
- 6-8: Gay Men's Health Crisis—Spring Card Program, 1997
- 6-9: Japanese American National Museum—Graphic Envelope, 1998
- 6-10: Japanese American National Museum—Plain Envelope, 1998
- 6-11a: Ronald McDonald House of New York, Inc.—No Teaser Envelope
- 6-11b: Ronald McDonald House of New York, Inc.—Teaser Envelope
- 6-12: Central Park Conservancy—Card Program Envelope
- 7-1: The Nature Conservancy—Acquisition Control Package Envelope
- 7-3: The New Democratic Party of Canada—"Hansard" Letter
- 7-5: The Arthritis Society of Alberta and NWT—Herrat Zahner letter
- 7-7a: Con Squire's "Sample" Letter
- 7-7b: Easter Seal Society of Ontario—Lapsed Renewal letter, 1994
- 7-8: Amnesty International Canada—DRTV "Light in the Darkness"
- 7-9: Canadian Cancer Society Manitoba Div.—Welcome Survey Sheet
- 7-10: Canadian Red Cross—Manitoba Flood Appeal envelope, 1997

- Organization Name
  - AARP Andrus Foundation (5)
  - AIDS Project LA
  - Amnesty International Canada
  - The Arthritis Society (2)
  - Bread for the World
  - The Canadian Cancer Society

- Canadian Diabetes Association
- Canadian Red Cross
- Central Park Conservancy (3)
- The Easter Seal Society of Ontario
- GMHC-Gay Men's Health Crisis (3)
- Japanese American National Museum (3)
- National Council of La Raza
- The Nature Conservancy
- New Democratic Party (Federal)
- Ronald McDonald House of New York, Inc. (3)
- Seva Foundation
- Smithsonian Institution NMAI (6)
- Sunshine Centre for Seniors
- TreePeople (2)
- United States Holocaust Memorial Museum (3)
- Con Squire's Sample Letter
- Three-year Scheduling Document

- Type of Organization
  - Education
  - Health
  - Civic
  - Social/Welfare
  - Government

Credit and Copyright

AARP Andrus Foundation (5)   Exhibits 6-5, 6-6, 6-7

    601 E Street, NW
    Washington, DC, USA 20049
    T: (202) 434-6190
    F: (202) 434-6483
    E: andrus@aarp.org
    www.andrus.org

AIDS Project LA   CD-ROM only

    1313 North Vine Street
    Los Angeles, CA, USA 90028
    T: (213) 993-1376
    E: deseasp@mail.apla.org
    www.reachout.org/losangeles/aids/aids01.htm

Amnesty International—Canada Division   Exhibit 7-8

    214 Montreal Road, 4th Floor
    Vanier, ON, Canada K1L 1A4
    T: (613) 744-7667 or 1 (800) AMNESTY
    F: (613) 746-2411
    E: info@amnesty.ca
    www.amnesty.ca

Amnesty International—UK Division   Exhibits 5-2, 5-3, 5-4, 5-5a,
                                                              5-5b

    99-119 Rosebery Avenue
    London, EC1R 4RE, UK
    T: 020 7814 6200
    F: 020 7833 1510
    E: information@amnesty.org.uk
    www.amnesty.org.uk

The Arthritis Society—Alberta & NWT Division (2)   Exhibit 7-5

    200-1301 8th Street SW
    Calgary, AB, Canada T2R 1B7
    T: (403) 228-2571
    F: (403) 229-4232
    E: info@ab.arthritis.ca
    www.arthritis.ca

Bread for the World   CD-ROM only

    #1000-1100 Wayne Avenue
    Silver Spring, MD, USA 20910
    T: (800) 82-BREAD
    F: (301) 608-2401
    E: bread@bread.org
    www.bread.org

Burnett & Associate (Jason Potts)   Exhibits 5-14a-g

    White Lion Court
    74, Rivington Street
    London, EC2A 3AY, UK
    T: +44 (0) 171-415 3333
    F: +44 (0) 171-739 0757
    www.burnettassociates.com

The Canadian Cancer Society—Manitoba Division   Exhibit 7-9

    193 Sherbrooke Street
    Winnipeg, MB, Canada R3C 2B7
    T: (204) 774-7483
    F: (204) 774-7500
    www.cancer.ca

Canadian Diabetes Association—Manitoba Division   Exhibit 2-4

    #102-310 Broadway Avenue
    Winnipeg, MB, Canada R3C 0S6
    T: (204) 925-3800 or (800) 782-0715

F: (204) 949-0266
E: mbinfo@diabetes.ca
www.diabetes.ca

Canadian Red Cross   Exhibit 7-10

1430 Blair Place
Gloucester, ON, Canada K1J 9N2
T: (613) 740-1900
F: (613) 740-1911
www.redcross.ca

Central Park Conservancy (3)   Exhibit 6-12

14 East 60th Street
New York, NY, USA 10022
T: (212) 315-0385
E: fayloga@CentralPark.org
www.centralpark.org/old/community/conservancy.html

Comic Relief   Exhibit 5-8

89 Albert Embankment, 5th Floor
London, SE1 7TP, UK
www.comicrelief.org.uk

The Easter Seal Society—Ontario Division   Exhibit 7-7b

#706-1185 Eglinton Avenue East
Toronto, ON, Canada M3C 3C6
T: (416) 421-8377 or (800) 668-6252
F: (416) 696-1035
E: info@easterseals.org
www.easterseals.org

Gay Men's Health Crisis (3)   Exhibit 6-8

The Tisch Building
119 West 24 Street

New York, NY, USA 10011
T: (800) AIDS-NYC
www.gmhc.org

Greenpeace International—UK Division   Exhibits 5-1,
                                                        5-6, 5-7

Canonbury Villas,
London, N1 2PN, UK
T: 020 7865 8100
F: 020 7865 8200
E: info@uk.greenpeace.org
www.greenpeace.org.uk

Japanese American National Museum (3)   Exhibits 6-9, 6-10

369 East First Street
Los Angeles, CA, USA 90012
T: (213) 625-0414 or (800) 461-5266
F: (213) 625-1770
www.lausd.k12.ca.us/janm/main.htm

National Council of La Raza   CD-ROM only

#1000-1111 19th Street, NW
Washington, DC, USA 20037
T: (202) 776-1790
F: (202) 776-1752
www.nclr.org

The National Society for the Prevention   Exhibits 5-9, 5-10,
of Cruelty to Children   5-11, 5-12, 5-13

42 Curtain Road
London, EC2A 3NH, UK
T: 071 825 2505
www.nspcc.org.uk

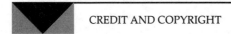

The Nature Conservancy   Exhibit 7-1

    #100-4245 Fairfax Drive
    Arlington, VA, USA 22203
    T: (800) 628-6860
    www.tnc.org

New Democratic Party (Federal)   Exhibit 7-3

    #900-81 Metcalfe Street
    Ottawa, ON, Canada K1P 6K7
    E: ndpadmin@fed.ndp.ca
    www.ndp.ca/www.npd.ca

Ronald McDonald House of New York, Inc. (3)   Exhibits 6-11a,
                                                       6-11b

    405 East 73rd Street
    New York, NY, USA 10021
    T: (212) 639-0100
    F: (212) 472-0376
    E: volunteer@rmdh.org
    www.rmdh.org

Seva Foundation   CD-ROM only

    1786 Fifth Street
    Berkeley, CA, USA 94710
    T: (800) 223-7382 or (510) 845-7382x300
    F: (510) 845-7410
    E: admin@seva.org
    www.seva.org

Smithsonian Institution NMAI (6)   Exhibits 6-1, 6-2,
                                                       6-3, 6-4,

    National Museum of the American Indian
    470 L'Enfant Plaza, SW
    Washington, DC, USA 20024
    T: (800) 242-NMAI
    E: NIN@ic.si.edu
    www.si.edu

Sunshine Centre for Seniors   Exhibit 2-3

    Box 849, Station F
    Toronto, ON, Canada M4Y 2N7
    T: (416) 924-3979
    F: (416) 929-8207

Tearfund   Exhibits 5-15,
                                                       5-16

    100 Church Road
    Teddington, Middlesex, TW11 8QE, UK
    T: 0181 977 9144
    F: 0181 943 3594
    E: enquiry@tearfund.org
    www.tearfund.org

TreePeople (2)   CD-ROM only

    12601 Mulholland Drive
    Beverley Hills, CA, USA 90210
    T: (818) 753-4600
    F: (818) 753-4635
    E: Treepeople@TreePeople.org
    www.treepeople.org

United States Holocaust Memorial Museum (3)   CD-ROM only

    100 Raoul Wallenberg Place, SW
    Washington, DC, USA 10024-2150
    T: (202) 488-0400
    www.ushmm.org

United Nations Association in Canada   Exhibit 2-1

    National Capital Region Branch
    #900-130 Slater Street
    Ottawa, ON, Canada K1P 6B2
    T: (613) 232-5751
    F: (613) 563-2455

E: info@unac.org
www.unac.org

World Wildlife Fund-Canada   Exhibits 7-2, 7-6

#410-245 Eglinton Avenue East
Toronto, ON, Canada M4P 3J1
T: (800) 26-PANDA
F: (416) 489-3611
www.wwfcanada.org

Con Squire's Sample Letter   Exhibit 7-7a

The National Copy Clinic
22 Lake Avenue
Auburndale, MA, USA 02466
T: (617) 332-2746

Three-year Scheduling Document   Exhibit 2-5
                                                             Appx. A-C

Michael Johnston
Hewitt & Johnston Consultants
#411-99 Atlantic Avenue
Toronto, ON, Canada M6K 3J8
T: (416) 588-7780
F: (416) 588-7156
E: info@hjc.on.ca
www.hjc.on.ca

▼ Index

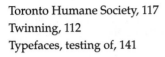

About the CD-ROM

For information about the CD-ROM see the **About the CD-ROM** section on page 177.